A must read! Stephane
Lord and wakens us to activate the Holy Spirit (the invisible
power of God) in our lives. As we turn the pages, the Holy Spirit
speaks to us as we see alignment within our own life situations
to reaffirm our faith in Christ and walk and live in the Word
of our Heavenly Father. Stephane writes from the heart. It will
transform you, strengthen you, and inspire you for more. It
moved my life, and it will awaken the warrior for Jesus in you!
—Nigel Edwards
President of OPSEU Local 565

The Ultimate Journey of a Warrior is a transparent and gripping
account of one man's life transformed through his desire to serve
God and how that became the driving force in all he would
accomplish. He recalls the intimate details of life-altering events
that could have driven him further from God yet served as the
foundation for an intentional, purpose-driven plan for his life.
You'll be riveted to every chapter. It had me questioning the
intensity of my own faith and its relevance to those around me.
It will serve as one of my benchmarks for how I choose to serve
in our current Christian culture. This book is a must read!
—MAK (Mary Anne) Moran
Author of *God Lives in Detroit (and Vacations in Other Places)*
and *Before I Knew You Loved Me*

I have known Stephane since 1995. He's a great guy and very
personable. We've shared many laughs, many tears, and many
disappointments together. This book will challenge you. After
reading it, being uncomfortable will become easier.
—Gary "Big Daddy" Goodridge
MMA Veteran, UFC Pride Fighting Championships, K-1
Fighter and Vale Tudo Champion, World Record Holding
Heavyweight Arm Wrestling Champion

If you spend time with Stephane, you soon realize that he's passionate about his faith. Stephane knows that only God can change a person's heart. Sharing from personal experience, he clearly shows readers that only Jesus can fill the void in their hearts. He will challenge you to go deeper and live a more disciplined life of following Jesus. Stephane loves to see people come to faith in Jesus and fulfill God's purposes for their life.

—Tom McIntyre
President, Reality Outreach Ministry

Luke 9:23 Love You Brother.

THE ULTIMATE JOURNEY OF A WARRIOR

A Man of God Under Construction

To my Brother in Christ Andrew. Thank you for Being Real. You are The reason why I am doing, what I am doing Today. I Believe in you Brother. Blessing

Stéphane Therrien

Your pal *signature* "warrior of God"

Printed in Canada

ISBN: 978-1-4866-1797-5

Word Alive Press
119 De Baets Street Winnipeg, MB R2J 3R9
www.wordalivepress.ca

WORD ALIVE
—P R E S S—

MIX
Paper from
responsible sources
FSC
www.fsc.org   FSC® C016245

Cataloguing in Publication information can be obtained from Library and Archives Canada.

We go to the gym to train hard, to do cardio, to bulk up, lean out, and achieve the perfect body. It is written in the Bible that physical exercise is good for us, but for everlasting results we should exercise ourselves to be godly. We should train our spiritual mind even more than our physical body. Are you in shape both spiritually and physically? Our body declines with age, sickness, and injuries, but faith in God can carry us through these tough times.

I have fought the good fight, I have finished the race, and I have remained faithful. (2 Timothy 4:7)

CONTENTS

ACKNOWLEDGEMENTS

I WOULD LIKE TO GIVE A very special thank you to my wife Karen (my G.I. Jane) for always believing in me. Thank you for your obedience to God, patience, grace, and faith in our creator. I'm still learning from you, especially with your actions and by the way you raise our daughter. Thanks for not judging me and for all your support, and of course for your great cooking. I love you so much.

To my miracle daughter, Chelsea Megan. I love you so much, Carebear. I love watching you grow to be a fine young lady. You are definitely a blessing from our Lord Jesus. Don't forget, always focus your eyes and heart on God and you will succeed. Do not let anyone tell you different. The proof is there.

To my mom and dad, thank you for bringing me into this world.

To my mentor, Pastor Bobby Thirsk. Thank you for helping me learn how to develop a relationship with God. You showed me how to be a good friend. There was never a wall between us. You always had time to fellowship and talk, with great listening ears, even late at night (with a coffee).

Nan and Pops, thanks for having such loving hearts, for your help and support in good and hard times. I am very blessed to have you as my in-laws.

To Jesus, our Lord and Saviour. Thanks for dying on the cross for us and forgiving me for being such a sinner. I love working for you, Lord.

INTRODUCTION

*Don't you realize that in a race everyone runs, but
only one person gets the prize … All athletes are
disciplined in their training. They do it to win
a prize that will fade away, but we do it for an
eternal prize. So I run with purpose in every step…
I discipline my body like an athlete…*
(1 Corinthians 9:24–27)

WINNING A RACE REQUIRES PURPOSE AND discipline. The
essential disciplines of prayer, Bible study, and worship equip
us to run with vigour and stamina. Don't merely observe from
the grandstand; don't just turn out to jog a couple of laps each
morning. Train diligently. Your spiritual progress depends upon it.

Your body is like a treadmill. You have to take care of it to stay healthy, to function well, otherwise everything starts to crumble and break down. You must have proper nutrition, sleep, exercise, friends, discipline, and self-control, or your physical health will go downhill. As we get older, our temple breaks down and we become weak like a child, so we have to focus on the most important health issue—our spiritual and mental health.

You were made by God and for God-and until you understand that, life will never make sense.

—Rick Warren

CHAPTER ONE

A BROKEN FAMILY

I will not fail you or abandon you.
(Joshua 1:5)

What we remember from childhood
we remember forever.
—Cynthia Zick

FIRST OF ALL, I'D LIKE TO say that I'm not worthy to do God's work. I'm only here to testify to his greatness. I was born in Sept-Iles, west of Labrador. It is sooo cold over there that Santa Clause doesn't even come … lol! When I was in Grade Four, in 1975, I returned home from school one day. All the ponds were frozen over and the other students were playing and sliding around on the ice. I joined in. After having some fun, it was time to make my way home. Walking back on the frozen water, the ice gave way under me and I ended up in the frigid water. I screamed for help, but all the kids left the ice, panicking.

A car stopped and a man pulled me out of the icy black water. I told him I was alright and later arrived home, soaking wet in –40°C. When I told my mother what had happened, she had no sympathy for me. Instead, I was disciplined quite severely. I guess Mom was scared of losing one of us, and she was probably under a lot of stress.

A few weeks later, Mom had to have a big surgery. She was hospitalized for more than a week. We didn't see our dad much at this time, when we needed him the most. He was a shift worker, but it seemed like we were seeing him less and less. I was just a young child when my mother said to me, "Your Daddy is gone."

"When is he coming back?" I asked.

"Sorry, Stephane. He is gone from our life. He has left us for another woman."

"But is he coming back tonight?" I asked, close to tears.

"Sorry. I wish I could say yes."

My mother hugged me and my sister Manon, who was too young to understand what was happening.

Even if my father… abandon me, the Lord will hold me close. (Psalm 27:10)

Being raised in a broken home can really have an impact on a child's life. Many have been forgotten or abandoned by a parent due to cheating or drug and/or alcohol dependencies. The effects of this can last a lifetime. But learn to trust in God, for his love for you can fill that emptiness and heal your pain.

The next weekend, my dad was to pick us up for a sleepover, and to meet his new girlfriend. I couldn't wait to see him. Since early morning my overnight bag, pyjamas, and toys were ready to go. When the afternoon rolled in, however, he still hadn't shown up.

Mom told us to get dressed and get in the car. "I'll drive you there," she said. "I will not raise the two of you by myself, I'll make sure of that." She was very angry. I was so sad.

Mom drove to where my father was living. His car was parked on the road. We waited, but not having a good knowledge of time at that young age, it seemed like we were waiting in the car all day. There was no movement anywhere. Even the streets were still. What a major disappointment! Our first sleepover was over before it even began.

A few days later, my father called and said that we would have a sleepover the next weekend. He would come pick us up for certain this time.

It was our first weekend away from our mother. It was an overwhelming rush to be back with Dad, but very strange to see another woman—another woman who wasn't my mother—hugging him. I received a present from him that weekend: a pellet gun. With it came many promises to go shooting empty cans together, but we only went twice and only for a few minutes.

Mom was a regular at the Sunday church service, and of course we had to follow. It was so boring for us. I couldn't understand when they talked about this man, Jesus. We couldn't see him, but he was supposed to be with us at all times? Try explaining that to a kid whose father has just abandoned him.

THE MOVE

Mom was unemployed, so it was time to sell the trailer we lived in. She just couldn't afford it. She began to work at a restaurant, and we moved into an apartment. What a complete change this was. We had a new school, new classmates, and new friends.

I had always received second-hand clothes from my Uncle Frank, strange clothes like bright red and yellow plaid pants. The type of clothes a clown would wear. When you're between ten and thirteen years old, that's not very cool with other kids. They definitely didn't want to hang around with someone who could be spotted five miles away. I got ridiculed a lot and bullied, as I was a tall skinny kid who was scared of my own shadow. I didn't have a father to reassure me or build my confidence. I still managed to make a few good friends over the years, though.

At age eleven, Dad registered me in the local hockey league. I was so scared of failure, so afraid to disappoint the people around me, that I always strived to do better. My work ethic was by far my best asset on the ice, but my talent was… well, not the greatest. My constant hard work helped make up for the lack of talent, let's just keep it at that.

I was a happy and positive kid and tried to fit in with whoever would accept me. That crowd of people didn't have my best interests at heart. I felt my dad didn't accept us, or that's how he was, so I was starving for attention from somewhere else, anywhere else. Neither parent came to my sports events very often. I would always see the same parents in the stands, but why not mine? I can count on two hands how many times either came to cheer me on or support me.

SOMEONE CARES

When I was thirteen, I was playing in a competitive hockey league, which involved going to different cities on the weekend for tournaments. We were able to get lodging from the parents of the other teams we played against.

In December of that year, one of my teammate's father, Mr. Gilbert, asked me where I was going to spend Christmas. He knew how mixed-up my home life was and he never saw my parents at the games to support or watch me. He also knew my dad wasn't in the picture too often.

"Stephane, I don't want to impose, but if you have no place for Christmas, come to our house," Mr. Gilbert told me. "I'll treat you like one of my own kids. You'll have a gift under the tree and we will fill up that growing body of yours. Think about it."

Wow. Talk about opening up your heart and home to a kid going to public high school, while his attended private school. I envied the lifestyle of my teammate, Dave, and how healthy and united his family was. I never took him up on the offer, but I have never forgotten it, either.

Living with my mom was beyond strict. Mom had a short temper, little patience, and lots of rules. I was so afraid of her. We were in bed by 8:00 p.m. every night, with the exception of some weekends. She was a control freak and overprotective. We didn't see Mom much, as she worked long hours, including split-shifts. Basically, we grew up without a mother or father figure. I became a very insecure kid.

She was trying to raise two children with little to no help from my father. I was disciplined a lot, and honestly, I probably deserved a few spanks, but I was growing and yearned for more freedom. I approached my mom a few times asking if I could begin training at the boxing club. She informed me quite firmly that she would not have any of that under her roof, and that she didn't want me to get hurt, again because she was so overprotective.

BROKEN HEART

At fourteen years of age, my dad asked me to consider moving in with him, his girlfriend, and her daughter. The main reason for this was that he wouldn't have to pay the child support for me anymore. I had some questions for him first. For instance, what was I getting myself into?

"Can I begin taking boxing lessons?"

"Yes," he answered.

"Can I have more freedom, come in a bit later, and not go to bed so early?"

"Of course," he said. "But we have to have a curfew."

"Can I still play hockey?"

"Of course you can."

"Can I have a girlfriend?"

"Sure."

Well, it doesn't get any better than that for a fourteen-year-old!

Whenever my mom and I had a disagreement, I always brought up that I was going to live with my dad. She always responded with "Go ahead, if you think you're so hard done by."

"Someday," I would respond.

I didn't mean it all the time. I loved my mom, but I missed my dad, too. I missed that man-to-man relationship, talking about guy stuff—you know… girls, sports, driving, and wrestling.

Eventually, I had to tell Mom that I wanted to try living with Dad. When the time came, I chose a moment when I was alone with her. I was shaking in my boots.

Here comes the bomb, I thought.

"Mom, I honestly would like to move in with Dad. I miss him, I'm fourteen, and I need him in my life. I want to start boxing and I know how you feel about that sport."

"Go ahead, if that's what you want."

From her voice, I knew I had just broken her heart.

"Can I come back if I'm not happy?" I asked.

"No," she said. "If you go, that's it. Your father can take care of you."

She really didn't want me to go. That's why she was being so harsh.

* * *

Moving Day began as a hot summer Saturday morning. I didn't have much stuff to move: some books, a shelf, clothes, plus a couple of personal items. Mom was sitting in her rocking chair, reading her book and acting indifferent to the whole situation. When I tried to talk to her, all I got in return were short, curt answers, and no eye contact.

There was a knock at the door.

"The guys are here, Mom," I said. Not a word from my mother.

Forty-five minutes later, all my belongings were out of the apartment. Throughout the time, my mother did not look up from her book once. For that matter, I bet she didn't even turn a page.

The moment when I left was awkward. I told her I was going to call her, but she just nodded, keeping her head pointed down at her book. Years later, I found out that she was holding back tears the whole time. As soon as the door closed behind me, my mother wept and wept, believing she wasn't a good mom. She questioned herself, wondering what she had done wrong to have things end up so badly.

Honestly, it had nothing to do with you, Mom. It was the decision of an unwise, mixed-up fourteen-year-old kid looking for his dad's attention.

> No matter how many books you read, no matter how many schools you attend, you're never really wise until you start making wise choices.
>
> —Mary T. Freeman

CHAPTER TWO

FANTASY WORLD

There is nothing so natural to man, nothing so
insidious and hidden from our sight, nothing so
difficult and dangerous, as PRIDE.
—Andrew Murray

"WHO IS THAT GUY YOU WERE talking to, Dad?" I asked.

"Bob Sirois, your boxing coach. You start Saturday."

As I walked into the boxing club, I couldn't believe the atmosphere. It had a cement floor. The smell of sweat, blood, and tears was everywhere. The mirrors were cracked. The canvas floor in the ring was stained with the dried blood and sweat of past fighters. The punching bags were held together with duct tape and hand wraps hung from the ropes to dry. It was a hardcore gym.

Soon I was making introductions, shaking hands with the guys who would be willing to hurt me by rearranging my face with bad intentions. I was impressed to see pictures of all the golden glove athletes I'd heard about on television and in the newspaper. Posters of past boxing events hung on the walls. Of course, I was dreaming that someday my picture would soon be there as well. My wish did come true, later on.

About eight experienced boxers were waiting in the coach's office, sitting on the floor, chairs, desk, or whatever was available. They laughed, bugged, challenged, farted and burped at each other. The room was brimming with testosterone, yet everything was relaxed and easy.

We heard the loud rumble of motorcycle engines outside, and when I looked out the window I saw two guys dressed in leather from head to toe, sporting their gang colours. They walked in, unshaven and very tough-looking. Right away, they saw my father and acknowledged him with a handshake. My dad introduced us. The first man was Reg, but nicknamed "The Fly" for his speed. The second man was Dan, or "The Kid," because he looked so young.

On our way out, The Fly said to my dad, "Hey, Denis. We'll make a man out of him."

"Yeah," my dad laughed. "I know you will."

The bikers also invited us to visit them at a nearby hotel bar, as they were both bouncers there at the strip club. Go figure. I spent many nights at the strip club, with and without my dad, whom I replaced with friends.

Praise the Lord, who is my rock. He trains my hands for war and gives my fingers skill for battle. (Psalm 144:1)

I was somewhat nervous for my first fight. I fought an exhibition match against a twenty-six-year-old, and it ended in a draw. I remember hearing the crowd with all their "Oooo's" and "Ahhh's," and I found it so awesome. Hopefully this would help me build my confidence—or was it pride?—and all the insecurities would melt away.

Because I lived in a small town, everyone knew everyone else's business—what they did, what they ate, who was dating who, and what they were involved in. At school, the other students began to treat me differently, with more respect and less teasing. In hockey, nobody would drop the gloves against me, because they had heard that I was now at the boxing club. I became very aggressive, always finishing my bodychecks on the ice.

Coaches from any sport almost always prefer a hard worker with less skill to a talented but lazy person, so I started to belong. Hard work has never scared me off. With more boxing matches under my belt, and the newfound respect from people around me, my insecurities were waning.

It started to go to my head somewhat. I was getting arrogant and cocky, two traits that I despise. Thankfully, I figured this out on my own and a good friend of mine confirmed it by the way I was talking to him. I later apologized to him.

SUMMER 1981

While off school for the summer break, I worked out every morning with Pierre, my hockey teammate and best friend. The rest of the day was spent biking around town or hanging out at the docks, suntanning. We were young and had no worries. We would reminisce about our workouts, and maybe if it wasn't too hot in the afternoon, I would head over to the boxing club and go a few rounds.

The odd Friday and Saturday night, I would go barhopping with Dad or a few buddies. At the age of fourteen, I looked much older than I was, and I was taller than most, so it was never a problem getting into the bars. Alcohol became a confidence booster. I was braver and cockier. Plus, I was with my dad. If I wasn't barhopping, I was up to no good, stealing bikes or experimenting with drugs.

GUN TO MY HEAD

One night I got chased by the cops. The police officer warned me to stop running. When he caught me, he pulled out his gun and pointed it at my forehead. I remember his exact words: "I'm sure you don't want a hole in your head." I will never forget those words or his posture as he stood in front of me with a gun. They brought me in for investigation and then released me with no charges around 3:00 a.m. It was my scariest encounter with the law.

I didn't like the high I was having, but I knew I was doing one thing right—I was attending church every Saturday night, mainly so that I didn't have to get up early and go on Sunday mornings with a headache or a hangover. Judging others became easy for me.

I had that big tree in my eye. I was blind to all my sin and probably the best lawyer when trying to defend myself. I was such a fake.

As a teenager, I liked to sleep on weekends… of course, what teenager doesn't? At church, I always sat in the back pews, so as not to be noticed or to make a quick getaway at the end. When I arrived, the priest would be greeting people with a handshake. But when he got to me, he would always say something like, "There he is. It's nice to see some young people walking straight and committing to the word of God." If he only knew what I was doing with my free time, he wouldn't have been so quick to give me praise.

Worshipping God once a week on Sunday isn't a relationship. Imagine only spending time with your spouse once a week and expecting your relationship to get better, or going to the gym once a week and expecting your body to change. We can't hear God because we're too busy with our personal schedules. We pray but we don't take time to pause in his presence. My actions in life didn't line up with what my tongue was saying, but going to church felt good. While I was there, I honestly felt peaceful and wanted to be a better person. I was going on my own and it was my decision, I just couldn't find that same calmness anywhere else.

WHY

Hold on, keep believing. Don't quit, don't give up. Let God do his work in you. The greatest tragedy is to miss what God wants to teach us through our troubles.

—Ray Pritchard

Suffering may be someone's fault or it may not be anyone's fault. But if given to God, our suffering becomes an opportunity to experience the power of God at work in our lives and to give glory to Him.

—Anne Graham Lotz

At the age of fifteen, my dad's girlfriend gave him an ultimatum, to choose between me, his only son, or her. That was an easy choice. I was his only son, his blood. Dad sat me down and told me his plan, what he was going to do.

"Steph, I know this is hard for you. It's very hard for me, too, but you've got to be strong. This is only short-term and I will go pick you up in a couple of weeks."

This meant my father was sending me to live with my aunt and uncle, who at the time had no children of their own.

"Soon it's going to be just me and you, living under the same roof," he promised me.

It didn't seem like such a bad deal. I was so insecure, craving for my Dad's love, that I agreed to whatever he said. He was my father, after all. I moved in with my Aunt Claudette and Uncle Aime. I had a very small room with a twin bed, no windows. It was about the size of a prison cell. I was not in prison, of course, and my aunt and uncle were extremely nice people. They acted like a second set of parents, but it just wasn't the same. Dad was a shift worker, so I didn't hear from him too often. I would receive a rare phone call at night and talk for two minutes or so. I was at school during the day and he worked at night. My uncle was so awesome, distracting me by playing mini-hockey in the living room. I always looked forward to that time with him. I believe he felt sorry for me, as he probably often heard me cry myself to sleep. I was lonely, scared, and insecure.

> God does not promise to keep us out of the storms and floods, but He does promise to sustain us in the storm, and then bring us out in due time for his glory when the storm has done its work.
>
> —Warren Wiersbe

Ever since I was little, my mother taught me to pray the Lord's Prayer. I began talking to God, one on one. Jesus was my friend, my confident, and I felt very much at peace with him. I would be sobbing, trying to be as quiet as possible, gasping for air and answers. I didn't know it then, but during those times when I felt so abandoned, God was with me. At the same time, I had so many questions for God: "Little baby Jesus, how can my dad abandon me—twice? What did I do wrong to make him act like this? Doesn't he love me?" In all honesty, my father did tell me that he loved me, and said it often, but his actions spoke louder than his words. Maybe that's all he knew.

Two weeks turned into two months, and after more than six months passed with me staying with my aunt and uncle, I moved back in with my dad—just the two of us under the same roof. He sat me down for a talk. I was very nervous. I hadn't liked the last chat we had a few months ago.

"Steph, I will never leave you ever again," he said.

I didn't care what happened in the past at that point. I was back with my dad, my friend, my drinking buddy.

THE SHOCK

In celebration of moving back in with my dad, some buddies and I got together for some drinks at my new apartment. Between four guys, we drank 132 ounces of liquor. After everything was gone, we stepped outside to go to the arena. From that moment on is a total blackout.

I woke up the next day at my mom's place with a major headache, very disorientated as to what had happened, and a little scared of being at my mom's, fearing her reaction. In all truth, I was shocked at Mom's kindness. She was tender and soft with me and never mentioned it again. The right side of my face was all cut up from a fall onto the curb. My mom told me I had been rushed by ambulance to the hospital with alcohol poisoning and a possible concussion.

What a horrible feeling it was to be robbed of all memory because of a choice I made, but it could have ended much worse. It was the beginning of my realization that consuming alcohol at the rate I was going was getting me nowhere fast.

Almost every day, Alain, a friend of ours, would stop by our apartment to talk and laugh. He was a couple of years older than me and had a promising career as a pro boxer. He had fought one of the famous Hilton brothers (Alex). The Hiltons were a well-known family of five talented knockout punchers, and they were coached by their own father, Davey Hilton Senior. Alain was a bouncer in a ladies nightclub (a strip joint). He had a short temper. He didn't like to talk much, and instead used his fists for conversation.

One morning while listening to the news, we heard that Alain was shot dead. It just goes to show that life in the fast lane—fighting, girls, drugs, and alcohol—can shorten your life, and quickly. I reflected a lot on what had happened to Alain, and knew it would be easy for me to follow that same path. It was time for me to make a decision to grow up. In the blink of an eye, what happened to my friend could have happened to any of us.

> The pages of your past cannot be rewritten, but the pages of your tomorrows are blank.
>
> —Zig Ziglar

CHAPTER THREE

THERE'S NO LIFE LIKE IT

The Lord is my light and my salvation
—so why should I be afraid? The Lord is my fortress,
protecting me from danger, so why should I tremble?
When evil people come to devour me,
when my enemies and foes attack me,
they will stumble and fall.
(Psalm 27:1–2)

Discipline is choosing between what you want now
and what you want most.
—Augusta F. Kantra

SINCE THE AGE OF FOURTEEN, I lived like an irresponsible single
adult. I was selfish, used alcohol and drugs, and I took advantage

of women. I was a cheater, liar, and thief… and I was very easy to influence. When I was sixteen, I had no excuse. Even without guidance, I knew the difference between right and wrong. At the time, all my choices seemed easy, even if they were not the right ones.

In order to be able to enjoy all my freedom, I needed some extra cash, so I took a job at the local McDonald's while in Grade Eleven.

One Saturday night, my father, a few buddies, and myself went down to a strip club to celebrate someone's birthday. This was becoming a ritual for us. Of course, it was no problem getting into the bar, since the bouncer, The Kid, was now a friend of mine. He and a boxing partner had taken me under their wings at the gym, teaching me the ropes.

Hours went by, all of us heavily under the influence of alcohol. My dad had had enough and drove home, so I took a cab later on. When I woke up on Sunday morning, I went outside our house only to find my father looking devastated. He was staring at his car, which had the right front bumper and panel all smashed up. Because he was so boozed up when he had driven home, he missed the corner, ended up in an embankment, reversed it, and kept on driving. He was fortunate not to have hurt an innocent bystander, or himself.

Monday morning rolled around, and I headed back to school to share my weekend triumphs and conquests. At school, we had a special visit from a military recruitment officer. I was so impressed by his confidence and the way he carried himself. He was extremely well-spoken and his uniform was crisp and sharp. I would never forget the medals hanging from the left side of his chest, shimmering in the light. His eyes connected with mine on many occasions during his selling pitch: "There is no life like a great military career, a life full of adventure and travel—see the world, be part of a team, earn a pension, keep fit and train everyday." He had captivated 100% of my attention. Instead of working in the mines all my life, I could become a soldier and finally obliterate my insecurities. At the time, it was the most important decision of my life.

THE HANDSHAKE

At supper that evening, I talked to dad about what I'd heard.

"Dad, you know, high school is almost over. You would like me to do something different than working the mines, right? In a few months, I'll be seventeen years old. I want to join the Army, but on one condition: you have to promise to stop drinking. If you so much as touch the bottle again, I'll quit the military and come back home to work the mines."

Dad extended his right hand and we shook on it. It was official: I was going to become a soldier in the Canadian Army. Dad kept to his word and became very seriously involved in Alcoholics Anonymous (AA). In turn, I became an Al-anon, a person living with and supporting an alcoholic. I also attended AA meetings to support my dad, and it sure didn't do me any harm in going.

I was getting very anxious to go to basic training. My head was spinning. I was already physically fit, but I didn't know what to expect. I would just have to go with the flow and face the storm for ten weeks of training. There was no backing down now.

THE GOODBYES

On November 3, 1984, I said my goodbyes. My dad was working that day, but I had already said goodbye to him. I had just two more family members to go. My mother and sister drove me to the airport. The twenty-minute ride passed in an uncomfortable silence, with only the minimum required conversation. I could feel their sadness in my heart. I hadn't lived with them over the past three years, and now I was leaving them again. My mom's baby boy was becoming a man, going off to represent his country in whatever situation he was thrown into.

My heart skipped a beat when I heard my flight number being called out over the speakers at the airport. I was scared and began to sweat. It was real. Manon threw herself at me, hugging me so tight, like we would never see each other again. She cried louder than the announcements on the speakers. My throat began to tighten up. I kept telling myself to be strong, but I was getting emotional. Suddenly, Mom lost it, too. She threw herself aggressively at me and wept. I felt the tears rolling down my cheeks and lodging in my mouth. Their faces were buried into my winter jacket. I still remember the sound of those heart-wrenching cries. Those were the most unforgettable hugs I have ever experienced. As I write these words, I relive that moment in my memory.

After a few minutes, I said, "Okay, I have to go." But nobody released their grip.

As I finally left, Mom said, "We will be praying for you. You are going to be alright."

I didn't respond. I was too heartbroken. I just gave them a small smile and walked away. Just as I crossed the gate to the plane, I turned back around to wave goodbye. My mother was holding my sister back with her arms around her chest. It was hard to let go, but it was an awesome demonstration of love.

BASIC TRAINING

What I am is what God has made me; it is a gift from God. What I become with it is a gift to God.

—Unknown

The flight to Montreal was peaceful and calm. I spent my time reminiscing about my life back home, all the Christmases shared, my family and friends. I didn't have much facial hair, and I knew we had to shave daily. The hair couldn't touch the tip of our ears. I had so many zits on my face, the dermatologist told me prior to joining that I wouldn't get any more pimples because there was nowhere left for them to grow … lol! My face did look like a dart board. Once I landed, I was bussed to what the Army called the "mega structure" in Saint-Jean-sur-Richelieu, forty kilometres southeast of Montreal. This is where they remould an individual in seventy days, making you into what the military wants you to be. But I knew even then that only God could change a heart.

I was exhausted from all the emotions and thought that I would just relax and get ready for my big day the next morning. Wrong! The bus pulled into an immense military training area, and as I disembarked a short, uniformed man with bad breath began screaming in my face: "Move, move, move... go, go, go... pick up your suitcases and give me twenty." I was nervous and caught off-guard, so I panicked. I reached into my wallet and pulled out a twenty. This, of course, only made him go more crazy; he had meant twenty push-ups. Wow! I was in his black book now, and the course had not even begun yet.

He was all over me at the debriefing until—and I still thank God for this one— another bus pulled up carrying a very drunk, loud, and obnoxious long-haired scuff. This other kid's attempts to stay serious were all in vain. He was so full of liquid courage that when three more uniformed instructors came up to him and started yelling, he burst out laughing. I knew then and there that they had their hands full with him. I would be off the hook for a while.

Day after long day, I wanted to quit. I couldn't handle the workload, the screaming, the stress, and I was desperately homesick. When times were overwhelmingly difficult, I would think of my dad. I had to keep going to make him proud of me, and of course for him to stay sober. A deal's a deal.

On Sunday mornings in basic training, it was mandatory to attend church. It was my quiet time with our creator. After ten weeks of gruelling training, I was a transformed man. What I mean by that is I learned how to get by on just a few hours of sleep, completing a large, demanding workload in a short amount of time. Learning teamwork is the only way to make things come together. I learned all sorts of new skills—ironing my clothes, polishing boots, bathrooms, and floors (yes, even with a toothbrush, just like the old story goes).

The platoon sergeant inspected everything in our 7 X 6 cubicle—from our uniform that had to be pressed with Spray Starch, helping it stay rigid just like hair gel, to personal hygiene. We had to iron a forty-five-degree angle on our bedsheet corner, also with Spray Starch. All the clothes had to be folded 12 X 12, exactly the same size as the floor tiles. Socks had to be rolled, and every item was personally stitched with our last name. We had an unimaginable number of chores that we had to accomplish as a team. Team work is what the army is all about.

On top of our personal tasks, we had to study, and nothing sunk in if you weren't in shape. We were so tired.

At seventeen, I had my own personal weapon—an old FNC1 that weighed a heavy eleven pounds. Everywhere we went our rifle had to be with us, and we had to name it like it was our girlfriend, because it also had to sleep with us. Later it was replaced by the C7 assault rifle, weighing 8.6 pounds with a thirty-round magazine. Helmet, webbing, rucksack, and sleeping bag were also part of the uniform. You had to fit all the necessary things into the rucksack and learn to pack tight and small. The rucksack weighed in at about seventy pounds with all your gear and a radio.

As part of our military training, we had to do a twenty kilometre walk with the full rucksack, helmet, webbing, and gun. Yes … good morning blisters. It really taught us team effort. Your fitness level was great by then, but first and foremost, you developed the attitude that you must go on, even when you can't go on anymore. Scrubbing the grout and toilet wasn't a joke; they had to be scrubbed with a toothbrush, just like in the movies, to get every little corner ready for inspection. All this was a game to mold us the way they wanted us to be and to see if we were going to break. If discipline wasn't your thing, military wasn't your future. If you couldn't follow orders from a superior, then you went back to being a civilian.

I also learned to eat on the run. Filling up my tray and having just two minutes to empty it usually meant eating as I walked from the pick-up line to the drop-off line. I had to walk through the gas chamber, watching guys vomit in their gas masks and wondering if I would come out of this alive. I learned precision weapon firing as well cleaning, assembling, and disassembling those weapons in the dark while being timed. I found out that the reason those massive cement fields are there is to conduct military parades, and the amount of time spent learning how to execute each move perfectly as a platoon is unimaginable, but very impressive to those who have the chance to watch. Sometimes we had to stand stiff on the parade square during a military drill for hours without moving. We could only move our eyes. Practicing this would help us at our post during war time, so the enemy wouldn't be able to see any movement. It became natural, but only if you had discipline. We were also taught advanced first aid and CPR to treat casualties of war.

Military soldiers are a special breed of human being— disciplined, strong mentally and physically, willing to go on minimal sleep and rations. Soldiers learn not to quit when it gets difficult, and they're flexible for any task ahead. When sworn in by the government, you become a soldier, and in time you move up the ranks. When soldiers print their names on a blank military cheque, it means they are willing to fight to defend their country at any cost. Don't forget, our *freedom* isn't *free*. They are also willing to sacrifice their life for their military brothers and sisters. In John 15:13, Jesus says that the greatest love is shown when people lay down their lives for their friends. That's exactly what Jesus did for *all* of us. Let's give all the love we can and try to give a little more.

The physical training was so demanding. The instructors wore white t-shirts and gym pants. I was impressed by their extreme level of fitness, being able to train platoon after platoon of soldiers so intensively, and yet they never seem tired. They kept going, going, and going, much like that little bunny from the battery commercials. I dreamed of one day becoming an instructor.

In addition to physical training, I had to attend a lot of classes about the military code of conduct and various rules. I was part of war games in the frigid night hours, running on little or no sleep while I carried my kit (ruck sac, weapon, ammo, food, clothes, helmet, sleeping bag, flak jacket) plus whatever other supplies were necessary, like the radios and stretchers. It would definitely have been more difficult for a smaller person, and harder on the women.

I was disciplined, independent, and in phenomenal shape. I felt like I could accomplish any task thrown at me. My insecurities had lessened, but I still lacked maturity.

On January 25, 1985, I graduated. My girlfriend of the past two years, my sister, and my dad glowed with pride from the bleachers during my military graduation. I was dressed in my dark green military uniform, boots polished like mirrors and buttons shone. My family was so impressed at how far I had come.

Following graduation, I was shipped out to CFB Borden in Ontario to receive career training. This was another three-month course, but not nearly as stressful as basic training—boot camp— had been. In the military, you are always taking courses to keep you sharp in your trade.

The military told us that if we were old enough to fight for our country, we were old enough to drink. Those rules have since changed. But I didn't miss a beat. I'd had lots of practice back home drinking. I had given up hope of finding relief for my inner aches. I was trying to escape in the fake, painful world of alcohol, numbing the harsh reality of life. I was blind to how I was destroying my life through my actions. The end results were always the same: no lasting fulfilment, just a major headache the following day.

I spent most of my paycheque on booze, which was my "god." I felt so empty in the morning when I sobered up. I don't know how many times I have driven drunk. My priorities were out of whack. I couldn't go forward. I always had negative resistance. Satan had a hold of me. Trying to find fulfilment without the Lord was like trying to play hockey without a stick. I believed in God, but I didn't honour him. I said I believed, but I was living as an unbeliever. My actions didn't follow God's teachings. If you *really* believe that eating well and exercising will help you stay healthy and lose weight or gain muscles, then you follow the program. I was like the Pharisees. I was honouring God with my lips, but my heart was far from the Lord. That's why the Bible is full of reminders to fear God.

HIGH TESTOSTERONE

The five-year relationship I had with my girlfriend ended in 1987. She was a lovely, respectful person who deserved someone who acted better than me. I was partying every weekend, but still going to church on Sundays to ask for God's forgiveness from my indulgent ways. Jesus was ready to change gears in my life, but I didn't want to commit for fear of losing out on something.

I was still training hard at the gym, doing both weights and cardio, and of course the occasional boxing. We were often confined to barracks—or, as we liked to call them, the shacks. We had to remain inside our rooms for study and inspections. It was terribly boring, so we organized boxing matches between different military units to kill time. We had no gloves in the beginning (just bare knuckles). The rules were to hit each other from the shoulders down to the hips; no head shots were allowed. Fists were flying left, right, and centre. Most guys had no experience or coordination, so they were getting pummelled fast. Some guys were actually running away! It was cheap entertainment, hilarious to watch. I could tell a few of them had some boxing experience, from the way they moved, bobbing and weaving, trying not to get hit.

Later on, we bought gloves and the rules changed to mirror a regular boxing match. Only a handful of guys would fight, because the head was the primary target. We had some courageous soldiers fighting out their frustrations from being cooped-up inside. Maybe they were angered from all the problems at home. We saw some funny knockouts, but there were no major injuries. Some of the guys needed to toughen up to be able to fight for our great country.

The boxing matches continued on a regular basis. When guys got frustrated with each other, they would come to our unit to borrow the gloves. Fighting was a much better way of dealing with their grudges than unleashing their wrath on each other with bare knuckles. Otherwise the Military Police would have been called in, charges would be laid, and guys could have gotten seriously hurt.

We are all fallen creatures and all very hard to live with.

—C.S. Lewis

CHAPTER FOUR

UNITED NATIONS TOUR

Though a mighty army surrounds me, my heart will
not be afraid. Even if I am attacked,
I will remain confident.
(Psalm 27:3)

IN SPRING OF 1990, I RECEIVED a memo stating that I was being transferred from CFB Borden to CFB Valcartier, with the Armour Corps—the 12th RBC (Canadian Armoured Regiment) Reconnaissance Leopard Tank. It was a six-hundred-man regiment leaving for a peacekeeping mission overseas during Operation Desert Storm—the Gulf War. It was called the computer war because of the air campaign. It was also known as the 1991 bombing of Iraq.

On a hot, sunny September day, the troops assembled in the hangar, surrounded by all the equipment to be shipped over with them. The base commander gave a speech of encouragement before the long flight, the start of a seven-month mission. It was time for final goodbyes. My best friend Pierre and my Aunt Sylvie and Uncle Camil (one of my dad's younger brothers, to whom I was very close) came to see me off and support me with hugs and words of encouragement. I was touched and knew that I would miss my friends and family so much, especially when I saw the next scene of despair. Children latched onto their fathers' necks, crying their little hearts out, not understanding why Daddy had to go away for so long. Those kids begged their fathers not to leave. They were just too young to understand. Wives hugged their husbands, knowing why they had to go, but hating to be left behind to worry. Some had rocky marriages, marriages that were about to crumble as soon as the soldiers stepped onto the aircraft. Parents said goodbye to their young sons.

I was surrounded by tears and broken hearts. Talk about a sea of emotions!

CHRONIC COMPLAINERS

I know from experience how hard our troops train, and what enormous expectations are placed on them, especially when they are serving on missions abroad. What really bothers me is when I talk to people who don't seem to care about Remembrance Day, November 11. They often say, "What's the big deal?" Some are quick to criticize our soldiers, wanting us to stay away from conflict, yet they may be at war with their own neighbour.

I often see bumper stickers stating: "If you are not willing to stand behind our troops, feel free to stand in front of them." I love it. You don't have to support war to support peace and freedom, and especially our soldiers. Be appreciative that we didn't have to fight for the enormous amount of freedom we enjoy. It was won for us. Canada and the United States are two of the richest countries in the world. We can walk into a health care clinic almost any time and receive care. We can go to a church and find out the truth of real love, God's love, without being beaten, stoned, or hauled off to prison.

We don't have guns pointed in our faces wherever we go. We have clothes on our backs and food on our tables. We have better job opportunities. We are able to marry people of different cultures without legally being beaten or killed. Complainers worry about natural disasters—earthquakes, hurricanes, fires, floods, homelessness, and poverty. They talk about it, but they do little or nothing to help. I'm sure they must have a university degree in complaining. They may fret about not having enough money, but they have a huge home, two cars, a boat, a motorcycle, you name it. They believe all the news on television, but not a word of the real truth found in the Bible. The weatherman tells us to prepare ourselves because a snowstorm is coming. People put their winter tires on and pull out their shovels and winter clothes. We try to warn them that Jesus is coming back, but they ignore us.

Where are our priorities? I once read a pamphlet that said: "In order to be among the wealthiest of the world, you really (by our standards) do not have to have very much. The research indicates that assets of just $2,200 per adult place a household in the top half of the world's wealthiest people. To be among the richest 10%, all you need is $61,000 in assets. If you have over the years gathered assets of more than $500,000, you're part of the richest 1%. There are approximately 37 million people that belong to this richest 1%. These numbers come from a United Nations study.

Maybe the body of Christ in North America should measure their personal wealth by comparing how many have less than themselves with those who have more. The truth is that half the world lives on less than $2 per day! Think about it. If it takes just a couple thousand dollars to qualify as rich, imagine what it means to be poor. There is no chance for these $2/day people to accumulate retirement savings. We are among the richest people on earth.

Often the debt we carry was created by wanting more, because we compare ourselves to our neighbours or friends. We want what they have; we envy and are never satisfied. The grass seems greener on their side, but under that green grass is dirt … like we all have. Just like we have skeletons in our closet, so do other people. I know … I was there … I was one of those guys. Sometimes I get caught wanting what other people have. By keeping my eyes on Jesus, I do have everything I need.

My point is this: be thankful for what you have. Instead of complaining and whining with a full stomach, reflect on what you have instead of what you're missing. Visit a third-world country— and I'm not talking about taking a vacation in a luxurious hotel. When you return home, if you still don't want to do anything to help, you are heartless.

ON HIGH ALERT

The tank regiment's duty while over there was to protect citizens. Within the regiment, I worked in the logistics field, supporting our troops. The only things to do in our free time was train and sleep. Lots of time we were thinking of home, what we would want to change about our lives on our return, what our families and friends were doing with their freedom. We watched the same movies over and over again. We watched *Cruising Bar* non-stop on VHS. We knew the movie from beginning to end. There was no internet to send each other email, nor were there text messages. We would always know the next scene in the movie we were watching and we would still laugh, sometimes even more because we were so tired.

When President George Bush Sr. declared war on Iraq with an air strike on January 17, 1991, all our priorities went from protecting innocent civilians with a 7:00 p.m. curfew. (No one was allowed on the streets after that time). Only the chickens and dogs were out. We were protecting our embassies against terrorism. As Canadian Peacekeepers, we were not involved in any dangerous missions. It was very different from the war in Afghanistan, a war which has resulted in hundreds of casualties— as well as many, many deaths. Our soldiers in Afghanistan were at war with complete cowards and terrorists. No one wins at war! I personally lost a friend over there. Families are destroyed, hearts are broken, children grow up missing their fathers or mothers. A friend of mine has done two tours now, and he has an incredible, heart-wrenching story of losing his comrades—and almost his own life—due to a roadside bomb.

THE SHACK

During the Gulf War, I didn't have the chance to see what was happening on the front lines. I asked my sergeant if I could go on a recce (reconnaissance) deployment walk to check it out, to see what the guys were being exposed to. Three of us were ready to go. We had flak jackets, helmets, and loaded C-7 rifles with the safeties on.

It was dark and cold. I couldn't see the shack until it was about twenty yards in front of me. It was the size of a twelve-by-fourteen shed with seven-foot ceilings. We turned the flashlights on as we walked in.

I wasn't really prepared for what I was about to see. The walls were full of graffiti and there was a large hole in the ceiling, the size of a garbage can. On the ground, beside an infant baby's chair was a hole about a foot and a half deep. In the hole was a bomb that hadn't exploded. It had just missed the chair. On the high chair tray was a small clay bowl with food that looked like pabulum (baby food) topped with dust and the remains of the ceiling, dinner table, and stove. I was stunned. I knew people had been eating here when the explosive came crashing down on their tiny home. Now imagine that it's your family's house.

When I got back to camp, I thanked God that I'd had the opportunity to see that with my own eyes. I was thankful for our country. I had stopped attending church since coming overseas—I only prayed, and usually just for things I wanted. After seeing the shack, however, I asked the military chaplain what time the church service was held on Sundays.

"I wish there could be a service, but no one ever shows up," he replied. "But if you're interested, what time is good for you?"

I told him that 10:00 a.m. was fine

He said, "See you at 10:00 a.m. on Sunday."

Now that was being obedient to God's duty (the chaplain, I mean).

Sunday came and I showed up with a friend of mine. Those services were my fuel for the week. Attendance only grew by small numbers, but listening to the chaplain preach the Word of God felt great! This was the same God I prayed to back home. He is with us everywhere. At these services, I felt like I was at home. Sunday morning worship was back on my list of priorities.

On February 28, 1991, at 0800 hours, President Bush ordered a cease fire after a successful ground campaign, ending the Gulf War. It was fought by the United States, the United Kingdom, Canada, Saudi Arabia, France, and Italy. Over 88,000 tons of bombs were dropped, and over 2,250 combat aircraft were involved, flying over 100,000 sorties. Tomahawk cruise missiles were launched from warships located in the Persian Gulf. Stealth bombers, F-16 and F-18 bombers dropped laser-guided bombs, destroying Iraqi and Kuwaiti armoured forces.

We can't forget the brave troops fighting on the ground and facing evil dead on. Their hearts were racing with a huge adrenaline rush. With many years of training taking over, they were acting on instinct.

The sacrifice we made was nothing compared to the previous war and the war in Afghanistan, where Canada lost over 150 troops. Their families are broken, hurt, devastated, and probably angry. Remembrance Day is a reminder and a celebration to acknowledge the ones who fought for our freedom. Freedom wasn't free for the many who dedicated their lives to fight evil.

Having a challenging day in Canada can mean:
- The garage door isn't functioning.
- The car broke down.
- My job isn't fun.
- I missed an appointment because of traffic.
- I have to work on Christmas or during a holiday.

A challenging day for a deployed soldier can mean:
- They don't know if they will return to camp after their shift.
- They lost a buddy in a roadside bombing or firefight.
- They lost a limb or are paralyzed for life.

It takes one second for a life to be destroyed and years to try to fix it. Many veterans are left behind in society without any support when they return home. Some become homeless. Canadian government, please stand up for our brave ones who gave us freedom.

You'll forget the heavy traffic that caused you to miss your meeting, but the soldier's scars remain forever from a lost limb, pain, depression, and PTSD. The war for them continues at home. Those are the worst wounds, when every day you relive in your mind those graphic images implanted in your head. You try to forget, but they keep hunting you down from the inside. It's a constant fight for recovery that seems to never end, with years of painful rehab. Many wounded soldiers that I know are so much more positive, appreciative, and happier than many civilians. The question is: Why and what are we complaining about? It all begins with *attitude*.

> The world will not be destroyed by those who do evil but by those who watch them without doing anything.
>
> —Albert Einstein

CHAPTER FIVE

DREAM JOB

And we are confident that he hears us whenever we
ask for anything that pleases him.
(1 John 5:14)

Success or failure can be pretty well predicted by the
degree to which the heart is fully in it.
—John Eldredge

IN 1989, I APPLIED FOR A career change, to a job that I would
still love to be doing to this day. I had always wanted to be an
instructor in the physical training department. It's something I
love to do. I had set my sights on this job ever since basic training,
after first seeing those instructors wearing the white t-shirts who
never seemed to run out of energy. Three years later, while serving

overseas, I received a memo confirming that in July 1991 my course would begin.

Part of the criteria of my new trade was achieving the rank of corporal, without which I couldn't be considered for the job of a PTI (physical training instructor). This job involved all aspects of the physical fitness training department. These were the men and women reshaping your body in basic training so as to be ready, physically at least, for military life. But I had to pass the course first, which was no easy feat. I was excited.

When returning home to Canada after my seven-month tour, my Aunt Sylvie and Uncle Camil picked me up from the airport at 3:00 a.m. I had two weeks off before returning to Base Borden for my course, and the beginning of my new career. I had the experience of seeing the joy and happy tears of soldiers reunited with their families, or soldiers coming back to a newborn they hadn't seen yet. It was such a blessing, just like those videos of soldiers returning home and surprising their families. Some came back to empty houses because their spouses had left them. That must have been a huge shock.

Coming back from deployment, I was seven months behind. I was still listening to the same cassette tapes on my yellow Walkman. Everyone else had gone on with their lives—new promotions, new jobs, marriages, and graduations.

Since I was a teenager, my Aunt Sylvie and Uncle Camil always treated me like their little brother and friend. They took me into their home and fed me. They weren't judgemental. We even vacationed together. Camil was like a father when mine wasn't around. He was such a clown, kidding and joking, and playing pranks. He always had such a huge smile on his face. Camil and Sylvie were a big support throughout the struggles in my life.

Camil passed away in the spring of 2009. When he left this world, I shed some of my biggest tears. To this day, I still cannot believe he is gone. I can still hear his laughter in my memories and I miss him more than words can say. I loved Camil very, very much.

The PTI course was six months of gruelling and intense training. We had the same schedule every day of the week. We also had to devise lesson plans at night. We swam many, many laps every morning, from 0730–1115 hours, just to warm up; the pool was twenty-seven meters long. This was followed by exhausting physical drills. During the last hour in the pool, we concentrated on water rescues, deep water rescues, spinal board injuries, packing and bandaging the patient, and performing AR (artificial respiration) in deep water. We had lunch from 1130–1300 hours, followed by classroom instruction. Imagine how difficult it was to stay awake for these very important lectures, after spending almost four hours of intense training in the pool and then filling up on lunch! From 1400–1500 hours, one student would present a sixty-minute lesson plan that was prepared the night before, consisting of one of the following topics: strength, cardiovascular training, circuit training, specific sport rules, or the refereeing of any sport. We practised our instructing techniques in front of a variety of military groups. From 1500–1630 hours, we ran eight to ten kilometres at a relaxed pace, or we would have four teams of six people practising military words of command (precise, short, loud instruction), running with and lifting telephone poles above our heads. We would do squats and stomach crunches with this immense piece of heavy wood. If we had poor teamwork, the shorter guys would end up in the middle with the tallest on each end, taking the brunt of the workload. It was a great exercise in patience, communication, drills, and teamwork, especially after the body was physically exhausted.

During the last month, we practised gymnastic manoeuvres to prepare for the graduation show, the moment we were all looking forward to. CFB Borden is a trades training base, and because I had completed courses there and lived there before, I was very familiar with the area. This was the base I would be posted to; it would become my home again.

This was honestly the best job I have ever had, life-guarding at the pool, being in the gym everyday, wearing gym attire as opposed to a regular military uniform, and training both military and civilian personnel. I got people in shape with military fitness testing, taking body fat index measurements on people and developing training and nutrition plans for individuals or sports teams. These were just some of the tasks my new job encompassed. I also trained the "Under 17" Canadian hockey team for three seasons, which was a very rewarding job.

I took many courses in both Canada and the United States in order to expand my fitness knowledge. Captain Dave Ogilvie, one of our physical instructors, was a hockey referee and a die-hard fan of the game. I guess I was in his good books. He always sent me away to do research whenever I told him that we needed to expand on the new training. He trusted me, and I'd come back with more scientific training methods to help our military personnel and athletics program. These courses exposed me to all types of training programs for athletes from strength training, plyometrics, cardiovascular, agility, power drills, nutrition, and more. Fitness is something I love to help people with, and gaining the best and most up to date information helped lead me to many other opportunities.

ANOTHER DREAM JOB

Dave also gave me the opportunity and privilege of training our new recruits for the JTF2 (Joint Task Force 2). All information was classified. This is our elite special operation force and counter-terrorism unit of the Canadian Armed Forces. They specialize in direct action, hostage rescue, and personnel recovery. I also had the privilege to train many NHL hopefuls, as well as NHL players. Two in particular stick out in my mind. They came from a family of three boys, all of them big. My knowledge was tested with those pro athletes. At this high level, they had seen all kinds of training techniques, so my challenge was to find ways to help them improve, because in fitness, if your clients don't see results, you're out the door. You have to work to improve yourself constantly.

Why do I say it was a privilege to work with these guys? Well, these brothers were very humble. Talented and smart, they would go out of their way to help anyone, especially young kids. They volunteered with other teammates to help at the hockey schools I organized for the local community. I developed a good friendship with all three brothers. The youngest, according to his two older brothers, was definitely the more talented and aggressive hockey player, but he chose not to follow that route. He became my training partner for a few years.

The two brothers who played in the NHL would come for training after the playoffs were finished. I trained them from that point until September, five to six times a week, and sometimes twice a day. I had to ensure they didn't over-train, so that they could get back to their respective team training camps and achieve peak performance.

Darryl Shannon was drafted as a defenceman by the Toronto Maple Leafs and then went on to play for the Winnipeg Jets, the Buffalo Sabres, the Atlanta Thrashers, and the Calgary Flames. He retired with the best hockey team ever, the Montreal Canadiens. Am I biased? Maybe a little … lol! His hockey career ran from 1988 to 2004.

His brother, Darrin Shannon, was drafted by the Pittsburgh Penguins as a left winger, and he went on to play for the Buffalo Sabres, the Winnipeg Jets (yes, the two brothers played together), and the Phoenix Coyotes. His hockey career ran from 1989 to 2000.

Over the course of one summer, one of the players, Darryl, helped me produce a hockey training DVD titled "What Every Hockey Player Needs to Do in the Summer to Be in Shape for the Hockey Season." This DVD of 127 minutes was given to the trainers of the Buffalo Sabres. They reviewed it and invited me down to gain some experience with the team during the 1996–1997 season. It was an awesome opportunity for me.

I stayed at Darryl's house for the time being. I also met and spent time with the knowledgeable strength and conditioning coach, Doug McKenney. I remember going to Sabres Land where they practiced and meeting all those young athletes full of testosterone. I felt like a kid in a candy store, meeting guys like the great centreman and Hall of Famer Captain Pat LaFontaine and goaltender Dominic Hasek, "The Dominator." That year they finished first in the NHL Northeast Division with a record of forty wins, thirty loses, and twelve ties, giving them ninety-two points. They lost the conference semi-finals to the Philadelphia Flyers 4-1. They played at Marine Midland Arena under coach Ted Nolan. From these brothers, I learned that no matter how successful you become in life, you can achieve the highest level of success by remaining humble. We're still friends today, and all of us have children now.

In the summer of 2000, I was invited to Jason Arnott's house. He was a hometown boy from Wasaga Beach, Ontario, who played for the New Jersey Devils. Jay scored the championship-winning goal in the second overtime of game six against the Dallas Stars. I'd met Jason the previous summer at the beach. He'd heard from a mutual friend that I was practicing the sport of Mixed Martial Arts (MMA). He invited me and Karen to come to his house and explain to him the rules of the UFC. That night I mentioned to him that if he ever won the Stanley Cup, he'd have to invite us to celebrate with them. If we had a child at the time, he'd have to allow me to put the child into the Stanley Cup. Ironically, the following season they won. I received a call from our mutual friend telling us that we were invited to celebrate with them. What a thrill it was!

———————

Don't be selfish; don't try to impress others. Be humble, thinking of others as better than yourselves. (Philippians 2:3)

Unfortunately, many of us have the desire to impress others by bragging about ourselves, both Christians and non-Christians alike. Being humble doesn't mean we are a doormat, allowing people to walk all over us. Rather, we are to serve others and treat them with the respect we all deserve.

———————

MY FUTURE WIFE

In 1995, I was instructing a gym class to about eighty military personal from Base Supply Company when my attention was drawn to one of the new girls. She was running around the gym floor with long blonde hair down past her glutes. She had blue eyes and was fitter than a whistle. I had never talked with her, but for me it was love at first sight.

Her group came into the gym for fitness training twice a week. When I wasn't instructing, I was by the window admiring how fit and beautiful she was, boasting to the guys I worked with, especially Dan Lefebvre and Rob Sneath, who himself was inducted into the Military Hall of Fame as a hockey player and, sadly, passed away recently: "Hey, look at my future wife." This, of course, brought about gales of laughter and teasing over my foolish thinking. All my coworkers, and some of hers, knew how I felt about her. I was on a mission, and when I finally talked to her, I was like a kid with butterflies in my stomach.

Karen began her military career on the West Coast in 1983 with the Air Force. She came from a good family, four kids in all, originating in Newfoundland. They were very easygoing and content people with strong family ties. They were always there for each other when needed; there was never a shortage of love or support. Karen was friendly and confident. She knew how guys were. She wasn't born yesterday, and neither was she easily impressed.

Having had made contact once or twice through work, I became brave enough to ask her out. I was hoping she would say yes, yet I was surprised when she did. We went out to dinner and a movie. By talking with her, I could see how kind and genuine she was. Karen became my steady girlfriend, and because she also believed in our Saviour we both started attending Sunday mass together. We were living in sin and had a very self-indulgent lifestyle. I often prayed about meeting a girl with the same interests, tastes, and healthy lifestyle as I had. I wanted her to love cooking and exercise, to adore children, and to be the kind of person others enjoyed being around. Most importantly, I wanted her to love God. Was I asking too much? Prayer gave me hope, and I really did believe I could conquer all my doubts through it.

In 1992, Karen became the first woman to be named Combat Service Support Soldier of the Year. She was also the first female supply technician to be posted with the Royal Canadian Dragoon Regiment, playing war games with the boys, running, carrying her weapon and rucksack, and doing unarmed combat training. I call her my G.I. Jane (like the movie). She served on two peacekeeping missions, one in Israel and one in Bosnia. During the peacekeeping tour in Bosnia, the former Yugoslavia, Karen's regiment came under attack. She was held hostage within the confines of her own camp. She jumped down from a sea container and injured her neck and shoulder in the process. Following a few surgeries, Karen was medically released from her military duty after twenty-one years of proud service to her country.

> Your times are in his hands. He is in charge of the timetable, so wait patiently.
>
> —Kay Arthur

CHAPTER SIX

GLADIATORS

When you go out to fight your enemies and you
face … an army greater than your own, do not be
afraid. The Lord your God, who brought you out of
the land of Egypt, is with you!
(Deuteronomy 20:1)

ALL MY LIFE, I HAVE CRAVED my dad's attention, a regular father-son relationship, probably even more since I joined the military. In 1995, I told my dad about this new mixed martial arts sport, UFC (Ultimate Fighting Championship)—caged fighting, for those who are unfamiliar with it. I started watching tapes of the sport.

In 1995, a guy I knew told me his friend was looking for a boxing partner, and had mentioned my name. Gary "Big Daddy" Goodridge was the Canadian Heavyweight Boxing Champion and a veteran of UFC 8–10. Gary became a legend in the MMA world. He was known as a knockout puncher and willing to compete at a moment's notice against anybody, anywhere. I became excited and nervous at the same time. We were both about the same weight, 250 pounds, so I responded "If he doesn't clean my clock, I would love to." Maybe that would get my Dad's attention.

I met with Gary, and my first impression was that he was a soft and well-spoken individual. It was hard to believe that this guy was bashing people's heads in the octagon. We talked about what he looked to accomplish, and at the same time how it would be good for me to learn a few things and travel the world with this new no-holds-barred sport. Working in a military gym, we had a tremendous amount of training equipment at our disposal. It became a fresh and challenging process for me to learn what was required to become a mixed martial arts fighter.

So I began a new era in my life, learning different fighting disciplines, like boxing, kickboxing, muay thai, wrestling, jui jitsu, karate, and judo. It became a 24/7 commitment, both mentally and physically. Training took place all over Ontario, and we sometimes went down to the U.S. to get the best training possible, yet I was still barhopping on the weekends, getting drunk. I was

There's so much worldly thinking out there today. Just like the Israelites, some days we may feel overwhelmed. Whether it be at school, work, or even among friends, we find ourselves totally weak and defenceless. Trust in God. He is more powerful than anything in this world.

more concerned about partying with my buddies and being popular than doing the right thing. Oh yes, I was still attending church with Karen on Sundays.

We had a fighting team of seven guys. One was an alternate from the 1976 Olympics in the freestyle wrestling. He was a Christian man; we could tell by his actions and the way he spoke. Other guys had experience with judo and karate. The smallest one was fast and talented, like Bruce Lee. Phong weighed in at a buck forty with fantastic ground submission, and he was as flexible as a rubber band. He was incredible in Ju-jitsu, submitting big men over twice his size.

I loved competing, and the science behind mixed martial arts fascinated me. Our team trained in the evening on Tuesdays, Fridays, and Sundays. All of us put on the wrestling shoes and wrestled, also working on jiu jitsu submissions for about ninety minutes on Mondays, Wednesdays, and Saturdays, but only Gary and I were going to boxing, kickboxing, and the muay thai gym. First we did rope-skipping, then shadow boxing, and we sparred for a few rounds. Our boxing skills, endurance, reflexes, speed, and cardiovascular became polished. The same thing happened with all the other martial arts disciplines we practiced. At the end, we would hit the target mitts or punching bag to attain final exhaustion and practice proper techniques.

They say that only practice makes perfect, but that's wrong; only perfect practice makes perfect. On my own, I also worked out with weights four times a week, averaging sixteen hours a week of fight preparation.

When I made the crucial decision to become more mature, my relationship with Karen became deeper, especially when I slowed down on my weekend binges with the boys and concentrated more on my fighting. She wasn't willing to put anything into a committed relationship until she could see something in me worth her time and effort.

> When you make a mistake, the time to make things better is now, not later! The sooner you address your problem, the better.
>
> —Unknown

CHAPTER SEVEN

UNANSWERED PRAYERS

The more you sweat in training,
the less you bleed in combat.
—Military Seal Team

IN THE SUMMER OF 1996, I broke my hand in training, requiring two surgeries. That fall, still full of piss and vinegar, I scheduled my first fight in Japan against Pat Smith, a veteran of UFC 1 and 2. Hopefully it would get my dad's attention.

I was extremely nervous, and as usual I became withdrawn. I was praying everyday for God to protect both me and my opponent from major injuries, so that we could have a good fight. But I was also asking God to put his favour on me. Unfortunately, the fight was cancelled due to my broken hand. I was so disappointed. I prayed everyday from that moment on.

On December 7, 1996, six thousand fans showed up at UFC Ultimate Ultimate, which took place in Birmingham, Alabama, Gary fought Don Frye. The top eight fighters of the year were gathering to have a chance to fight three times in one night for a purse of $50,000. On the card was the legendary Ken Shamrock, Tank Abbott, Don Frye, Kimo Leopoldo, Gary Goodridge, huge Paul Varelans, Cal Worsham, with Steve Nelmark and Mark Hall as alternates in case someone got hurt or couldn't go on to the next fight. Both alternates had a chance to compete. The final was between Tank Abbott (runner up) and Don Frye (winner), who fought three times that night.

Art Davis, the president of the UFC at the time, told me after watching my resume on tape—demonstrating strength, submission, and boxing techniques—that I would be fighting February 7, 1997 in Niagara Falls, New York at UFC 12: Judgement Day. I couldn't wait to tell Karen and my dad so that they could watch me on pay per view.

For those who don't know what UFC fighting is, let me explain. At the time, it was a no-holds-barred sport with little or no rules. The fighting took place in an octagon thirty feet across, totalling 750 square feet, and surrounded by a six-foot chain-link fence. There was a referee, gloves were optional, and it was a kicking, kneeing, punching, elbowing, head-butting, hair-pulling, bone-breaking type of fight. The only rules at the time were no eye gouging, no mouth fishing, and no biting. The only way to stop the fight was by knockout, referee stoppage, or tap out (giving up). If need be, your corner could throw in the towel.

Let God do his work in you.

The greatest tragedy is to miss what God wants to teach us through our troubles.

—Ray Pritchard

During MMA training camp, you will get hurt, 100 per cent for certain, or at least someone on your team will be injured. As you pursue training, you feel that pain because you keep pushing forward. Your jaw can't open well from being hit, your legs are like hamburger meat from the kicks, your ribs are tender, and to top it off, you're covered with cuts and bruises. You verbalize that you're hurting and that you can't go on, but then your team says, "We're all in pain and hurting." It's so true, because *everyone* is hurting in different ways. The moral of this story is that the way we react will make all the difference for us and our surroundings.

Life isn't easy. I consider the trouble we go through to be a blessing from God to help us in life. Often God will use our pain to teach us something. Let me be clear that the Lord doesn't want us to suffer, but he will use it to help us grow. Often that pain keeps us humble, teaches us patience, exposes our weaknesses, destroys our pride and ego, and makes us kneel down and look up to heaven for comfort.

This happened to our daughter. We often tell Chelsea that her toughest opponent will be herself. She was competing once in downtown Toronto at a Taekwondo tournament. She was on her way to the gold medal when she reinjured her right ankle while kicking. She had to fight two rounds of ninety seconds each, and she was still in the first round. She didn't want to cry in front of the crowd in the arena, but she had to kneel on one knee because the pain was atrocious. The crowd became quiet, waiting to see what would happen next. The doctor came to wrap her ankle, and then she looked at us, hoping we'd tell her to stop, but she already knew that in life you find a way to keep on going, even if it's hard. When it's difficult with your spouse, you keep going and find a way to fix it. If you're sick, kick yourself in the butt, get up, and go to work. Life is what we make of it. God doesn't create garbage. We are his precious children.

My wife, Karen, looked at me, and in a loud voice I said to Chelsea, "You are doing good, Carebear; you are strong and courageous. Remember what we taught you—find a way to finish the race ... *fight!*

She got up, wiped her tears, and kept on fighting by using her other leg and more punches. She fell down a few more times from the pain, but *she never quit.* The crowd encouraged her and her opponent to no end. She received great applause for her courage. We were ecstatic parents to see the strength God gave her. She was carried to the podium by her coach to receive the silver medal. To this day, Chelsea is happy that we pushed her to finish the tournament strong. She gained lots of respect from her teammates, and they knew when sparring with Chelsea in training that she wouldn't quit.

If we don't take time to be physically fit and healthy, we'll have to take time to be physically sick. The same applies to our spiritual life with Christ. If we don't eat well, don't exercise, and go to sleep late, we're writing a recipe for disaster. The same applies to people who call themselves Christians. We can't just go with the waves; we have to be disciplined and apply the scriptures.

I often stumble, but I pick myself up, repent, and race to the finish line. In MMA, I have trained and sparred with UFC champs/contenders. Some of these guys are scary just by looking at their resumes. They are the best of the best. I travelled everywhere to get the best training and learn different fighting styles. I was disciplined, with countless hours of training to be better, stronger, faster, and more dangerous when fighting. I practiced the same techniques a thousand times so that they'd come naturally to me. I was healthy physically but my spiritual journey with Jesus was less desirable. My spiritual life was last on my priority list. I was so vain. I wanted perfection, but not the kind of perfection I was created for. All my energy went to the gym.

My faith wasn't growing, and we know why—I didn't apply myself. I was spiritually dead. What if I travelled the world and learned at different conferences and Christian men's events? What if I applied myself to be a better father, husband, and warrior of God? What if I spent as much time with God as I did at the gym? What if I learned the scriptures and read them a thousand times over, like I worked on my martial arts moves? It would also come naturally. They say that what we do the most shows where our heart is. Do you agree? Please don't watch from the sidelines. Get involved doing what you're called to do. We can be close to Jesus … it's our choice. I encourage you to change your priorities if need be, one step at a time, and get closer to God. It's the only hope we have.

Karen was very supportive, and although she still worked full-time in the military, she found time to cook seven healthy meals a day, as well as training with me and Gary at the boxing and kickboxing club. She also helped me train other athletes of all types. She was honestly my biggest supporter. We were not yet married and were living together in sin. We both knew Jesus, but did not yet have a relationship with him.

During the Christmas season, Gary and I went to Michigan to train with Dan "The Beast" Severn, and also to attend his fight against Mark Coleman at UFC 12. He was the main event to the card I was also competing in. Once again, the fight was cancelled twenty-four hours prior to the tournament and moved to Alabama. It was cancelled in New York State because the rules were not tough enough. State regulators wanted the fighters to wear helmets and gloves; gloves were optional and helmets were not worn. To top it off, a few weeks prior, my doctor told me I wasn't fit to fight, as my hand still hadn't healed properly. I kept on training hard in the hopes that God would give me an opportunity to fight.

To everything there is a season, a time for every purpose under heaven. (Ecclesiastes 3:1, NKJV)

In the spring of 1997, my third fight was scheduled in Kanawaga, Quebec on the Indian Reserve, as it was still illegal everywhere else at the time. This time, I was fighting Big Harry Mascowitz for $300. He was a construction worker, 6'5", and weighed in at 300 pounds. He was also a UFC veteran. Harry dropped out one week before the tournament. I talked with the fight promoter and he told me had two different styles of fighters for me. Great! At least I was still fighting.

Then, four days before the tournament, after asking the fight promoter once again what fighter and what style I was up against he told me the news: "The Canadian government will lay charges against anyone organizing or fighting in this event." Here we go again! God must have had different plans for me.

March 31, 1997, was my last day in military uniform. I officially retired after thirteen years of active duty to my country. The federal government was disbanding my trade, as a physical education recreational instructor, and filling the PTI position with university students, paid half the salary I was making.

God was still looking out for me. I had an interview to work at the gym, still as an instructor, and I got the job. I even kept the same desk and was training the new university apprentice with the military fitness class. I was still able to live in the military housing with Karen, which helped us financially, and I continued to train hard, travelling all over to get as much fighting experience as I could.

Gary was still active with his agent, who was finding him fights in Japan. Now we were training for Kimo Leopoldo, an Evangelical Christian from Hawaii who was preaching the Gospel wherever he went. I was looking forward to meeting this guy after cornering for Gary at Pride Fighting Championship Tournament

#3 in Yokahoma. I had first encountered Kimo, a very colourful and ferocious fighter, at UFC 11.5 in Birmingham, Alabama and in Pride Fighting Championship #1 while cornering for Dan "The Beast" Severn.

A couple of days before leaving for Japan, I did my ritual of going out with the boys for a few beers. Early the next morning, Karen woke me up. "Gary is on the phone, and he says it's urgent," she said. The conversation went something like this:

"Why are you calling me so early?"

"Listen, I just talked to my agent and Kimo is out"

"What do you mean out?"

"He's flying back to the States as we speak to get knee surgery," Gary said. "He got hurt in Japan during his training session."

"You're kidding, right?"

"No. Listen to this, my agent got you a fight in Japan for $7000, with 10% of the purse going back to the agent."

"Against who?"

"Me," he replied.

"Really?"

"What do you think?"

"I'll call you back in two minutes," I said. "I'll talk to Karen first."

Karen was happy for me, but had mixed feelings about me fighting my training partner and friend. I called Gary back, accepting, and told him to keep his chin up. We laughed.

Gary had been trying to get me fights with his agent since we had started training together. With only a few hours of sleep, I hung up the phone. I was walking on cloud nine.

I put on my walkman and went out for a hard run. I had so much energy! I was visualizing the fight and praying for no bad injuries for either of us. I had been training with Gary for the past three years, so I knew he was a stand-up fighter, just like me. Both of us were ready to bang.

Gary had four years of ring experience. I knew I was going to have more jitters than him and maybe make a fatal mistake. I knew the huge Japanese crowd would be behind him. Gary won most of his fights by knockout. In training, we never KO'ed each other. The boxing gloves were sixteen ounces, versus four-ounce MMA (mixed martial arts) gloves, but I could end up lying face down on the canvas. Sunday morning, on our way to the airport, I didn't show my feelings to him, but I felt like throwing up. Gary had been knocking out people left, right, and centre on the biggest mixed martial arts stage in the world.

We travelled with Carlos Newton, one of the original MMA pioneers and Pride FC Japan MMA legend and former UFC welterweight champion, and his coach, Moni Aizik, an Israeli-born martial artist. He was also the founder of commando Krav Maga (a military self-defence fighting system derived from street fighting). We had some good times and shared good laughs.

This was my second trip to Japan, and when we arrived we were greeted by Japanese translators and Gary's agent. I got hit with a major disappointment right away, as they told us they didn't want me to fight Gary anymore. Kimo's training partner was still there in Japan and he had agreed to fight Gary. That was my fourth lost fight opportunity. It had been so close to happening. I was already there, but I did feel some relief after the announcement. I knew that this must have been God's plan all along. What is it that He wanted to teach me?

I cornered for Gary and he won by knockout in the first round. Amir Rahnavardi was Kimo's training partner. I had breakfast the next day with him. He said that he wanted to throw up as soon as he agreed to take the fight. He took some good blows, got knocked out, but was okay. Nice guy to talk to.

Months went by and no tournaments were on the schedule, but we still trained hard, trying to polish our submissions, stay healthy, and improve our cardiovascular (at 250 pounds, you huff and puff pretty quickly). The training was always much more difficult than the actual fight. Most of the time in the heavyweight division, fights ended in knockouts.

I was still going to church with Karen. It had become a routine more than anything else. On occasion, I would go out with the boys on the weekends for a few cocktails.

Often I have made a request of God with earnest pleadings even backed up with Scripture, only to have Him say "No" because He had something better in store.

—Ruth Bell Graham

In spring 1998, I got another fight opportunity in Kanawaga, Quebec, on the Indian Reserve. This one was a go. I had my ECG and EKG (heart and head tests), plus my HIV test done. I had ten weeks to prepare, and again I prayed everyday for God's protection.

As fight day (May 2) got closer, I got a lot more quiet than usual in the house. I was mentally gearing up for the tournament. I was nervous. I did not have any big conversations with Karen, and thankfully she knew me well enough by then not to start any. I focused and visualized every second of the fight, round by round, in my head. I saw myself in the worst position and fighting through it.

When May 2 arrived, and you guessed it, I still could not fight. I had not received the results of my HIV test on time. My prayers were never answered (at least, not the way I wanted) for competing in mixed martial arts, but God's promise still holds today. He will protect me.

Yet you don't have what you want because you don't ask God for it. And even when you ask, you don't get it because your motives are all wrong— you want only what will give you pleasure. (James 4:2b–3)

Ask God in prayer for His will to be done, as opposed to your own wants. Trust God to fulfill all your needs

I was taught that sometimes God doesn't answer our prayer because of barriers such as:

- unconfessed sin—Isaiah 59:1–2
- unforgiveness—Matthew 6:14–15
- disobedience—1 John 3:21–22

Before we pray, repenting removes all obstacles to a straight line to our Lord. And don't forget, God knows our needs.

Financially, I was struggling. As a civilian instructor on the base, I only had half the military salary I was accustomed to. I would never be able to buy a house on my own. I was living on peanuts with a small military pension. Two weeks following the final fight, I received a call from my doctor regarding my HIV test; the results were negative (thank you, God). Two hours later, I received a job offer at Honda of Canada Manufacturing, beginning in July. The job offered twice my current salary. God has His time for everything! Thank you, Heavenly Father, for unanswered prayers. If I would have fought, maybe I would have gotten hurt badly, jeopardizing this great opportunity.

I was still able to become a volunteer firefighter for fourteen years. It reminded me of the team work offered by the military. I still had fighting on my mind, though, so it was back to the drawing board. I kept on training, waiting to see what God had in store for my future.

> You don't know precisely what you need—or when you need it—but God does. So trust His timing.
>
> —Unknown

CHAPTER EIGHT

MIRACLES HAPPEN

Children are a gift from the Lord;
they are a reward from him.
(Psalm 127:3)

IN DECEMBER, KAREN AND I WERE given a trip to Cuba by some NHL friends I was training. What a surprise and what a gift! We were so humbled that others thought so highly of us. It was time to go shopping for a ring … yep, a ring! In my mind, I was going to ask Karen to marry me in the plane. I was going to arrange the big proposal with the pilot and the stewardess. If Karen said no, then I'd never see all those people again once we landed. I chickened out.

While in Cuba, I proposed after dinner one evening to her in front of four hundred people. I was so nervous, but I wanted to spend the rest of my life with her. Believe me, her "Yes" was a big relief. I'd bought a rose to replace the box for the ring. When she'd open the rose, the ring would be beaming.

I had it all worked out with the staff at the resort. They were playing a game on stage, and I'd arranged for them to call Karen and me as the last couple to participate. The entertainer pointed his finger at us to come and play. I was saying no, but Karen said, "Come on, it will be fun." She had no clue. We climbed the stairs to the stage, and then the entertainer handed me the microphone behind Karen's back.

I knelt down, and when she turned around she was in shock. She put her hands in front of her face in disbelief. I began my little speech of about thirty seconds and asked her to marry me. She cried non-stop for about three minutes. I was clenching my teeth, waiting for an answer. Then the entertainer took the microphone from my hand and asked the question again for me: "Is that a yes?" Karen nodded her head and said yes. I was sweating bullets. I became the luckiest man that day.

On June 24, 1999, we bought a house in Barrie, Ontario, outside the base. We worked hard to renovate it the way we wanted, but Karen wasn't feeling well. Karen was diagnosed with a brain tumour in 1989 and was seeing a doctor on a regular basis to ensure it wasn't growing. She was having nasty headaches that made her vomit, and she had to rest. The doctor told her to begin examining other ways of having a child, like adoption, if we were at all interested, as it would be impossible for her to conceive and carry though a pregnancy.

So we began the process of looking first in Canada, then different countries and cultures. As we continued the renovation, Karen's parents were nearby to help. Her family was always there when we needed them. To this day, they are so awesome.

Karen was beyond exhausted. Her schedule was so full, from training soldiers during the day, teaching extra fitness classes in the evenings and during lunch hours, and following her own personal fitness program. And, of course, there was the house to think about. She was a runner, and never tired of it, but lately she couldn't run long distance without getting tired after a few minutes.

I was working the afternoon shift at Honda Manufacture, and before work I trained on base at the gym. Every day Karen would drop by to say hello before heading back home.

One day, she worried me by stopping by the gym and walking straight towards me. The look on her face was so serious. I knew she had gone to a doctor's appointment that morning, so I knew I had to be very supportive. Maybe the tumour had grown…

"Hey babe, how are you doing?" I asked.

"Okay," she replied with a little smile.

"How is your head doing?" I asked a bit nervously.

"Oh, my head is okay."

"What did the doctor say?"

Her smile grew larger. "He said that we are at least sixteen weeks pregnant."

"What?" I was shocked

"Yes, you heard right."

"Sixteen weeks… how can it be? The doctor told us to start adoption… and where is your belly?"

"God always has the last say," she told me.

I wasn't ready to argue that point.

"So that's why you've been so tired all along," I said with a laugh.

"Yep."

I gave Karen a hug and a kiss. I was stunned by the great news. I had mixed feelings, both excitement and fear at the same time. I went around the gym and told everyone.

What you put into your child's heart today influences their character for tomorrow.

—Author Unknown

On February 2, 2000, Karen gave birth to our precious little miracle baby girl, Chelsea Megan.

A girl! Oh no, what was I going to do? I had a daughter now. I became very scared, thinking about the girls I had dated in my past, how I'd hurt them with my words and actions, how I'd lied to them just to get close. I had done it all to hide my own insecurities. Everything I did in the past to those girls was now going to haunt me. All those girls were somebody's daughter, just like my baby. I wanted to protect Chelsea from all those dirty boys! All fathers probably felt the same (I hope) about young, immature, irresponsible punks, like I had been.

RAISING A POSITIVE CHILD IN A NEGATIVE WORLD

My child, listen when your father corrects you. Don't neglect your mother's instruction. (Proverbs 1:8)

If we don't teach our children who God is, someone else will teach them everything that he's not.

—Darlene Schacht

If you demonstrate a great fear for spiders, chances are your child will be afraid of spiders, too. If you show love and respect for our Lord Almighty, again, chances are your child will as well. Our actions always speak louder than our words.

Parenting is a touchy subject under our roof. I want to make sure I'm equipped with all the necessary ammunition for our daughter's daily battle. Being a parent is so challenging. I missed out on this growing up. My parents thought they were doing the right thing by working long hours or keeping themselves busy, but they were not with us. My sister and I grew up craving attention and love, any kind would do.

Since Chelsea's birth, I haven't wanted to commit those same mistakes. I attended dozens and dozens of seminars on Christian parenting and read lots of books on the subject. One study I participated in at a local church was based on the book *Effective Parenting in a Defective World*, by Chip Ingram.[1] I am still learning, and I pray daily for strength, protection, guidance, and wisdom… and not to screw up. My parents lacked so many parenting skills, and I did not want to fall into the same trap.

[1] Chip Ingram, *Effective Parenting in a Defective World* (Carol Stream, IL: Tyndale House, 2006).

Many parents believe that since there is no divorce in their home, there are no parenting problems, yet they don't want to participate in activities that may not interest them, not realizing it is for the children to experience, not for their enjoyment. I have asked fathers from my church and at work to join dads on the same journey. I am so shocked when they decline the invite. They say, "Maybe next time." Sadly, this lack of involvement shows by the way some of the kids crave attention and love.

Here on earth, you have to become the role model and the hero in your child's life. Make sure that they follow Jesus' example first. Our kids are more important than any activity we're involved in. Anyone can be a father, even animals. In the summer of 2017, I discovered six baby rabbits behind our house. The male rabbit had planted his seed, but he didn't stay to help raise them. To be a dad takes time, commitment, and dedication, even if you have to change your plans. We have to make sure that our kids come first.

As dads, we have huge responsibilities, accountability, and modelling to do for our children. The job must be taken seriously, like it or not. Our prisons are full of fatherless men and women who needed a dad.

Men, let's take our responsibilities seriously. If you lack on one point, make it right today. I'm learning daily, and I have to work on myself every minute to be a better dad also. When you become a dad, it's forever.

I hear it and see it because I was there once before. I can see myself as a young boy in my kid. That's where I need lots of grace. Seeing these parenting deficiencies is a trigger point for me, and if

I'm not careful I can become quite angry. I have to remember and repeat the words of Proverbs 29:11:

Fools vent their anger, but the wise quietly hold it back.

I saw firsthand what lack of attention and poor parenting did to my sister and me. I remember the sinful paths we took, because of our own choices and the poor guidance we received. That's why now I choose guidance from the scripture, because scripture teaches us parenting the way it was intended to be. Chelsea learns about Jesus by the way we express our love to her. We hope our guidance will teach her the path God wants her to go in life.

The best way to raise Chelsea is to live well and let her watch us. I haven't seen perfect parents yet, so our kids can't be perfect either … right? Kids don't listen too well, but they're watching everything. We use words to build Chelsea up instead of words that diminish her. I know that society will try to tear her down, because our society is hurting so much. Everyone wants to be accepted and gain approval from others.

Jesus is the only approval we should crave. Once I was craving worldly pleasure because I wasn't fulfilled, and I always ended up disappointed. After getting that promotion, that raise, the new car, the vacation down south, we wait for the next high. The world is a wheel of disappointment. How many sick people do we know who are actually happy? Honestly, the only ones I know are followers of Christ. They have hope and know where they're going next.

Some of you may have doubts, so let's look at this together. What if God is real and you didn't give him a chance? What if you lived by your own standard? Then everything is lost. If he's not real, then you've lived a good life and been a positive example for others … and you haven't lost anything. We may choose to live our lives without Jesus, but we can't spend our eternity without him. We have to sincerely think about that before we put a wall up.

> Being a good father is like shaving. No matter how good
> you shave today, you have to do it again tomorrow.
> —Reed Markham

I know I am the first man in my daughter's life to give her unconditional love, so I have to set a high standard. She needs this vitamin called "love" from me. Love is the secret for a healthy, spiritual upbringing. We spend time with our daughter, telling her with both words and actions the love we have for her. We build her confidence by listening and interacting with her, making her feel important and special. I tell Chelsea how proud I am of her, giving her words of encouragement.

Most importantly, I show my daughter what love looks like by how I talk about Jesus and the way I treat her mother, my wife, with the utmost love and respect. She can see the playfulness we share together, the way we pray and play together, and hopefully she can see later in life to never settle for anything less from her choice in a husband. Many Christian books on parenting say that every dad should take his daughter on a date regularly (maybe once a month), each child getting some individual one on one time. These dates don't have to be expensive outings. All you need to do is pack a lunch, and surprise them with a picnic at lunch time, picking them up from school. Or maybe just go out for some fishing, or walking along the lake. Most kids don't care what they do with you, so long as you want to do something with them.

> Far too many parents are more interested in their kids making the team than making the kingdom.
>
> —Dr. Tony Evans

Our priorities often get mixed up. We think that being successful means making lots of money by working long hours, which come at the expense of neglecting our families. We all know the saying: "Work to live, don't live to work." My identity isn't based on my work, but I give my all at work. That's where we're mixing it up, and you can see it in the world today. Kids are looking for their parents' attention … or any attention.

Being at work too long can become a trap that will hurt your family. Co-workers told me once that they work long hours because they don't like to be at home. Maybe if we work on our relationships with our spouse and put in as much effort as we do at work, going home will be awesome. Don't let the enemy convince you to let your work come between you and your family. The more money we have, the more things and worldly pleasures we buy. Do your best at work, but don't let it jeopardize your home.

I validate myself by being a successful husband, dad, and follower of Christ. There's always room for improvement.

We have to be involved with our children, helping our daughters to learn how to properly interact with boys. We need to teach our daughters to hold a conversation socially, especially while on a date, and teach our sons how to properly treat and respect young women. This is important because when the conversation ends and they don't know what else to say or do, it is then that they may end up in the back seat of the car, where a lack of judgement could forever alter their lives. We are responsible to educate them to guard their hearts, minds, and bodies. Just talking to our children isn't enough. What kind of legacy are we leaving behind?

If you want to know where you stand in the lives of your children, ask them what they think about you, your positive and negative points. Tell them to be honest. If any faults go against God's teachings, you have some homework to do. For me, I have learned to apologize when I'm wrong, to show her that I know I'm not perfect. If we never apologize when we should and feel no remorse, our insecurities and pride take over. In those times, the Holy Spirit is not in us.

> In this world, I may just be one person, but to my daughter
> I may be her entire world.
>
> —Author Unknown

I don't want to be an irresponsible dad. It takes time, patience, and 100% commitment to raise a child. It is important for my wife Karen and me to have social conversations with our daughter every day at the dinner table. We ask Chelsea what she worked on in school that day, what positive and negative things transpired. For teenagers who are working, the same thing applies. We all need communication and dialogue with our kids. We get her to go into detail, so that she is capable of explaining things well. Participate in activities that interest your child, even if they are not your favourite. You may be surprised at just how much fun you will share and how many memories will be built. After all, our children are gifts from our creator.

Direct your children onto the right path, and when they are older, they will not leave it. (Proverbs 22:6)

It's good to raise them according to the scriptures, but don't forget to choose the right path also. The Word of God isn't only for our children; it's for all of us.

TO DADDY, LOVE CHELSEA

With the help of my wife, Chelsea made me a Father's Day gift—a box with pictures of me and her on top, with hearts all over the sides. It is very colourful and decorated inside and out. It was very light. When I opened it, it was empty. Where was the present? I thought she had forgotten to put it in, so I asked her, "Is this a special box for Daddy to put stuff into?"

Her little face was glowing with pride as she answered, "No, Daddy, it's a box full of kisses. I blew kisses into it until it was full. Now every time we are not together and you're missing me, just open the box and take out as many kisses as you want, and when it's empty, I'll refill it."

It is my most treasured gift from my daughter.

With my eyes brimming with tears, I knelt down and gave her a big hug and a kiss. She was so proud, and I felt truly blessed to have such a wonderful relationship with my beautiful girl. I still have that box in my nightstand.

Dear children, let's not merely say that we love each other; let us really show the truth by our actions. (1 John 3:18)

Live fire training

With my daughter Chelsea before her high school prom.

Live fire training at base Borden, being my daughter's hero.

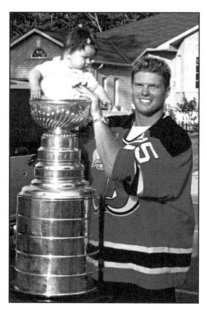

*My little "Care Bear" Chelsea, celebrating in the
2000 Stanley Cup with Jason Arnott*

Me and my wife Karen (G.I. Jane) serving overseas.

Dedication, hard work, sweat, and blood, equal ready for battle.

The legendary "Big Daddy" Gary Goodridge, Moni Aizik,
Carlos Newton (former UFC champion), Myself

Me, Gary, and UFC hall of fame Dan "the beast" Severn. After a
successful tournament of fighting in Pride 1 Japan.

"Warrior of God"

Vacationing and enjoying the heat with my wife.

This is the Outreach Truck that we use to bring the necessities of life to our less fortunate/homeless.

Emmanuel's Wish Foundation. Bobby and I bringing sick children for medical aid in South Africa.

In the slums of Nicaragua feeding families.

*These hard working people live at the dump, collecting plastic and steel,
barely making $2 a day, per family.*

CHAPTER NINE

MANMADE RULES

*But there were also false prophets in Israel, just as
there will be false teachers among you.*
(2 Peter 2:1a)

A FEW WEEKS WENT BY AND we settled down with our new little miracle baby. On one particular Sunday morning, we were on our way to church to fill our Sunday obligation. It was Chelsea's first time.

There was a blizzard outside, the roads weren't ploughed, and we could hardly see anything in front of us. When we finally arrived at the church, the limited parking lot was already filled, and due to the snow parking on the road was

---

There is a lot of information out there today promoted by false teachers. Take care to really check it against the one true authority: the Holy Bible.

not advisable. The church service had already begun and people were still entering the building—late, unfortunately, due to the weather.

As we walked into the church, the priest was telling the congregation, "Don't arrive late. God wants you to be on time. Don't leave early. Stay until the end of the service, and don't park in the front or we have you towed away."

Everyone in the church was looking at each other in awe. I don't know how much we missed prior to coming in, but people were still coming in late and surprised about the speech. In a way, the preacher was right. We say, "Jesus, you're so important to me," but we're regularly late *once* a week going to church service. However, we're always on time for work, which is provided by the Lord. If I go to a movie or sporting event, I'm always on time, and I *love it* when it goes into overtime. If the preacher goes over the time limit, I look at my watch. I had to look deep inside my heart and find out where I'd placed God on my list of priorities.

We had to re-evaluate where we were headed, spiritually, with our newborn. We had been attending this church since we moved to Barrie. There were too many manmade rules for our comfort. The church twisted scriptures to meet with their own interpretations, and they couldn't back up many of their rules with teachings from the Holy Bible. In the end, we stopped attending church altogether.

Don't get me wrong—the church was teaching biblically, but we didn't know if the preacher was telling the truth all the time because we didn't compare his sermons with scripture. We didn't even own a Bible. Our problem was that we didn't have a relationship with God. We were religious. We were looking for approval from people, not God. We were following rules instead of Jesus. We'd listen to the message from the pulpit and feel great, but as soon as we walked out the door, we forgot it. We didn't apply it.

Not everyone who calls out to me, "Lord! Lord!" will enter the Kingdom of Heaven. Only those who actually do the will of my Father in heaven will enter. On judgment day many will say to me, "Lord! Lord!" We prophesied in your name and cast out demons in your name and performed many miracles in your name." But I will reply, "I never knew you. Get away from me, you who break God's laws." (Matthew 7:21–23)

Going to church and fellowshipping with believers is needed, but serving the Lord is what we're here for. We can serve him anywhere, not just in a church assembly. We can serve with a pure motive of a humble heart, and also from where we're at on our personal journey with Jesus. Stay vigilant in prayer and scriptures and ask God for wisdom.

It seemed like we were arguing and nipping at each other more and more. We were paying no respect to our Heavenly Father, leaving us unfulfilled. We needed God back in our lives, but we couldn't expect God to show up in our lives in a dramatic way if we didn't show up before him in consistent and faithful ways. There's a big difference between knowing the truth and living for the truth. We didn't apply the scriptures as we should have.

The only way we can find real satisfaction is by having a relationship with God. Realizing that now, I see that all my achievements only made me happy for a short time. Once reality would sink back in, I'd be back wanting more, unsatisfied once again.

I was one of those believers … I believed in Jesus, but I didn't follow his word of truth. As a Christian, I honestly feel at peace now, walking with Christ and doing what he says. The Bible is the best moral story ever lived. I believed, but I never read scripture and rarely prayed. Now I read and thank Jesus in good and challenging times. As a believer, I was only talking about my faith when it was comfortable to talk about it. Now I share my faith openly. As a believer, I didn't sacrifice much. Sorry … I didn't sacrifice anything. After everything Jesus sacrificed for us, truly following him requires daily sacrifice. That's what the Word says. I believed, but I also followed the world. Now I've learned to rebuke temptation. If we really believe, we should really see the fruit of it, right? I will go deeper and explain later.

On June 24, 2000, Karen and I tied the knot. We were finally married. I know we didn't put our family together in the order God wanted us to, but we really didn't rely on God that much at the time. We thought we could do it on our own. Looking back now, we can clearly see how Christ was absent from our life.

In spring of the following year, a co-worker told me about a new, hip, and loud Christian church that he and his wife attended on Sundays. He described it having a very relaxed and fun atmosphere. He said, "There are people at the door welcoming you in, people talking with each other, and people introducing themselves if they notice you are new. The church itself is not uptight, and the dress code is 'come as you are.' The pastor is on fire for God and quite entertaining. The music really helps you get your heart into the worship as people sing, dance, clap, and lift their arms up to the Lord. They have many small groups to help address the needs of our community. They also have home Bible studies. It's honestly pleasant going to church to worship God."

It sounded so inviting and full of energy.

Going to church doesn't have to be boring; it should be a celebration! It certainly would bring a lot more people in the doors to hear the Word of our everlasting Father.

I often trained at the local gym on Sunday mornings. On many occasions, I was working out with a guy named Bill. Well, four weeks after I was told about this new church, Bill and I were pushing some iron together.

For, there is only one God and one Mediator who can reconcile God and humanity—the man Christ Jesus. (1 Timothy 2:5)

There are no statues, dead saints, or any other person who advocate to God on our behalf other than Christ Jesus.

"Do you go to church?" Bill asked.

"Well, we haven't gone in quite a while. We didn't like the way the church was run. It seemed to us that some of the religious leaders believed that their manmade rules were equal to God's laws. First of all, if you are not of their denomination, you are not saved or going to Heaven. The Bible never mentions denominations; it talks of Christianity, serving God with all your heart, mind, and soul, 24/7. That's what the Bible talks about, not different denominations."

Their worship is a farce, for they teach man-made ideas as commands from God. (Matthew 15:9)

Knowing something by heart, or acting exactly how you are supposed to, is not enough. To God, our actions must be sincere.

Along my journey I have realized, both in combat and fighting, the importance of having brothers around you. Not brothers who are exactly the same as you, though, or else you will not have a well-rounded troop. As I have grown as a believer, I have seen a sad thing in the splintered body of Christ. Many Christian denominations tend to keep us from fellowshipping with one another. We can easily look down on other believers who don't believe just as we do rather than value them for who they are in Christ. We are one body. To be strong, we need to look for reasons to include other believers, not exclude them or just focus on their differences.

Just as our bodies have many parts and each part has a special function, so it is with Christ's body. We are many parts of one body, and we all belong to each other. In his grace, God has given each different gifts for doing certain things well. of us the ability to do certain things well. So if God has given you the ability to prophesy, speak out with as much faith as God has given you. If your gift is serving others, serve them well. If you are a teacher, teach well. If your gift is to encourage others, be encouraging. If it is giving, give generously. If God has given you leadership ability, take the responsibility seriously. And if you have a gift for showing kindness to others, do it gladly. Don't just pretend to love others. Really love them. Hate what is wrong. Hold tightly to what is good. Love each other with genuine affection, and take delight in honoring each other. (Romans 12:4–10)

I am not trying to offend anyone, but before we make a statement about a church or judge another person's faith, we have to recognize the difference between Christian principles, church traditions and manmade rules, and the scripture of the true Word of God. That is why we have so much division and confusion within Christianity. Maybe we should learn, read, and study what the Bible is teaching us about adding or removing words.

And I solemnly declare to everyone who hears the words of prophecy written in this book: If anyone adds anything to what is written here, God will add to that person the plagues described in this book. And if anyone removes any of the words from this book of prophecy, God will remove that person's share in the tree of life and in the holy city that are described in this book. (Revelation 22:18–19)

So I chose to follow God's Word, not man's opinion. It is our duty to learn what the Bible teaches us.

Now, God has a sense of humour. It turns out that Bill attended this new church I had been told about by my coworker, and he began to describe it in exactly the same way.

> The church is not made up of spiritual giants, only broken
> men can lead others to the cross.
>
> —David Bosch

"Someone told me about your church," I said to Bill when he was finished. "Maybe it's another hint from God. You know what, I will go next weekend. After all, Karen and I have nothing to lose."

Our relationship was missing God, and we were sinking without Him. Karen was more sceptical than I was. She questioned anything she didn't understand, which in the end (when we gave our hearts to Jesus) made it all the sweeter. The whole atmosphere was different than what we were used to, yet it was so important to us both to find a home church to raise Chelsea in.

Non-Christian friends ask me why I go to church when it's full of hypocrites. I tell them: "I need to work on myself and be better than I was and become less of a hypocrite. Jesus has removed many of my bad habits. I didn't believe it would work, but it did. That's why I keep going. I feel at peace with people striving to do better spiritually.

"I also go to the gym just like you to work on my flaws and stay healthy physically. Many unfit people go to the gym to get better. Not everyone applies themselves at the gym, and it's the same at church. Let me know if you ever want to come and I'll pick you up."

And let us not neglect our meeting together, as some people do, but encourage one another, especially now that the day of his return is drawing near. (Hebrews 10:25)

When going to church, it may not be the message from the pastor you draw strength from, but the love and support of your fellow Christians.

The moment I stepped into that new church, it felt right. I felt so much peace. I knew we had found what we'd been missing. For the first time in my life, I had no worries and I felt so much joy. I wept without understanding what was happening, I felt so good. And I didn't care if anyone was watching me! It is hard to explain; you just have to experience it for yourself.

The pastor asked everyone to bow their heads. Then he said, "If you have never made a decision to follow Christ, if you have never asked God into your heart , then today could be the most important decision of your life, to accept Christ as your Saviour and Lord."

Going to church, giving to the poor, and being religious does not save you. You are saved only when you invite Christ to come into your life. It is a gift from God to anyone willing to accept it.

All of us will die someday, and at the end, you have to ask yourself where you want to spend eternity.

With our eyes closed and heads bowed, Karen and I held hands as the pastor spoke. We prayed this simple prayer of salvation: "Lord Jesus Christ, I ask you to come into my life and forgive me of all my sins. I confess my sin before you this day. I denounce Satan and all his work. I confess Jesus as the Lord of my life, and I ask you to come into my heart right now. I confess with my mouth that you rose from the dead. Write my name in the Lamb's book of life. I want to serve you, Lord Jesus, from this day forth. Thank you for saving me. In Jesus' name, amen."

We become saved when we accept Christ as our Lord and Saviour. We have to believe that Christ died for our sins and that he rose again; it's part of salvation. This means to accept him as Saviour. But Christ as our Lord is only part of it. Accepting Christ as Lord means giving him *Lordship* over our lives. This goes beyond just believing in him and accepting his forgiveness. It means giving our lives completely to him. (If we really believe, we will follow.) This allows Christ to rule over our lives. Both parts, Christ as Lord and Saviour, are important to salvation.

> We do not need to put our house in order before Jesus comes in. He puts it in order after we let him in.
>
> —Unknown

After my salvation experience, my life was still the same. Nothing major changed, except for the joy in my heart; it was bigger than any happiness I had ever experienced in my life. I wanted to be surrounded by other believers like me, to see if they felt the same way I did.

Although others may say they felt no big change at the time of their baptism, I did. I was washed clean and ready for any battle. When I was alone, I was *not* alone. I would talk and share my feelings with Christ, because I knew he was listening. My Christian brothers and sisters would pick me up with words of encouragement when I was feeling down, without judging, because we were all on the same journey together. Even with life's struggles, my conversion didn't just change my life; it also changed the lives of the loved ones surrounding me. If Jesus can change a man like me, he can change anyone. No man's sins are too big for God's forgiveness.

Look! I stand at the door and knock. If you hear my voice and open the door, I will come in ... " (Revelation 3:20)

In the past, I had been a lost sheep, controlled by lies and alcohol, which I used to escape the reality of this evil world. I was lost by insecurity and doubts from my old demons. From my research, the word Satan means "adversary or opposer, enemy of God

_____

The temptations of this world—money, power, possessions—will stay here when we die. God promises eternal peace and satisfaction. Jesus loves us and wants us to accept this gift, but it is our choice to open the door to our heart and let him in.

_____

himself, the people and purpose of God." The word devil means "slanderer or accuser."

Above all else, guard your heart, for everything you do flows from it. (Proverbs 4:23, TLB)

Prior to being in God's army, I thought I could do everything by myself. Talk about arrogance! God gave me my 6'2", 250-pound frame, which was strong on the outside but fragile on the inside. In an instant, I was washed clean with hope.

A friend once told me that being a Christian is just like being a pumpkin. God picks you from the patch and washes off all the dirt. He scoops all the bad seeds from inside you—the doubt, the hate, the selfishness, the pride, etc. He puts his light inside you to shine for all the world to see. Wow! How can you not be tempted by Christ's free love? After all, happiness comes and goes. Buying a new car or a new home, or having a new girlfriend, only lasts a short time.

The joy you experience inside by knowing and having a relationship with God is unexplainable. Just like walking on the moon, you have to experience it to know how it feels. I know Jesus carries me through the trials and tribulations I face daily. Doing it alone is never easy, and often more painful. I give him all my worries and problems. I didn't just make God a priority in my life, I made him the *centre* of my life. I surrendered everything into his hands. That's what he wants us to do: rely on him, for he created us.

Satan continues his effort to make sin less offensive, heaven less appealing, hell less horrific, and the gospel less urgent.

—John MacArthur

Life isn't always groovy and easy. God never promised it would be. He promised to be there to comfort and carry us through the hard times, giving us peace of heart. But non-Christians have a close eye on us and expect us to be perfect. They will try to mislead or distract you from your joy, which you can only find in Christ. These lost souls will often try to deceive you or remind you of your past to confuse you.

Only fools say in their hearts, "There is no God" (Psalm 14:1).

So we become foolish or wicked, not wanting to live by the true Word of God. Scripture also says that "*fools despise wisdom and discipline*" (Proverbs 1:7). We want to do it on our own without guidance and direction. Funny, I was that guy. I can understand their pride, but I was proven wrong.

The enemy of God accepts the world we live in, including divorce, adultery, pornography, abortion, greed, and self-righteousness. The list could go on and on. Former President of the United States Ronald Reagan said, "I've noticed that everybody that is for abortion has already been born."[2] I sometimes feel like the enemy is prowling around, looking to steal and destroy what I have found with our peacemaker. But when you are with Christ,

---

[2] "Ronald Reagan, Quotable Quote," goodreads, accessed October 23, 2018, https://www.goodreads.com/quotes/116615-i-ve-noticed-that-everyone-who-is-for-abortion-has-already.

the only thing Satan can do is put doubts in our head. The more we fill that space with our everlasting Father's love, the less room there is for corrupt thoughts and bad intentions.

Remember, Satan is the ruler of this world. Kenneth E. Hagin uses the word "HALT" to help shield yourself:

H – Never get too hungry.

A – Never get too angry.

L – Never get too lonely.

T – Never get too tired.

Satan will try to sway you over using any means he can. The one sure way to get him to back off is the name of Jesus.

So humble yourselves before God. Resist the devil, and he will flee from you. (James 4:7)

In my fighting days, I got a tattoo in Japanese lettering which translates to "NO FEAR." These words have taken on a new meaning, that with God I truly have no fear. I can face the biggest of obstacles. The pain is still real, but I can feel him carrying me in difficult times.

MORALS

Have I now become your enemy because I am telling you the truth? (Galatians 4:16)

We say that we want honesty, but it seems that we don't want to hear the truth. The way we say it to others should be the way we'd like to hear it ourselves. I'm still working on this one, and I fail many times. If we stay humble, put our pride aside, and are willing to learn, it's easier to swallow. Not too many people gain popularity by telling the truth.

Canada and the United States were built on strong Christian principles, and because of that God blessed them with more riches than any other country in the world.

The world we live in today began to go down the drain in the mid-1980s. The world has changed faster in the last thirty-five years than in the previous nineteen hundred years. Everything seems to be accepted and legal. Why is our world becoming more destructive?

The answer is simple: we are removing God and prayers from our homes, schools, and government offices. Is it because the Bible says we shouldn't lie, steal, or kill, and that we have to love our neighbours as ourselves? Is it that bad? We have become our own god, but the Bible is still the best message for our moral standard.

And you will know the truth, and the truth will set you free. (John 8:32)

So we won't be deceived by the lies everywhere. Our society is inundated with porn, prostitution, drugs, blaspheming, sexual sin, misuse of the Lord's name, and hatred. A great amount of music and movies are about raping and killing, and we worship pro athletes and celebrities but get mocked if we worship God, our creator. We don't cheat anymore or commit adultery; instead, we say we made a mistake. We're afraid to say "Merry Christmas," so now it's "Happy Holidays." Schools teach kids about sex, even explicit sex. What happened to the days when they taught abstinence (refraining from sex)? Now they sell condoms in schools and call it "prevention." People are getting divorced left, right, and centre. The prisons are fuller than ever, and fathers aren't taking responsibility for their families.

Being politically correct doesn't mean you're morally right. If it's wrong, it's wrong. Just because it's legal doesn't make it moral. Never forget that!

> A lie doesn't become truth, wrong doesn't become right, and evil doesn't become good just because it's accepted by a majority.
>
> —Rick Warren

Just because we disagree with others doesn't mean we hate or judge them, or that God loves me more than them. It means that our opinions are also valid. Statistics say that we have many experts on our planet, but our world is still going to mush. People have made the choice to live without God, so we shouldn't complain that our world is falling apart.

Anne Graham, the daughter of evangelist Billy Graham, has been asked on a number of occasions how a good God could allow something as awful as 9/11 to occur. She's explained it this way: "I would say for several years now Americans in a sense have shaken their fist at God and said, 'God, we want you out of our schools, our government, our business; we want you out of our marketplace.' And God, who is a gentleman, has just quietly backed out of our national and political lives, our public lives, removing his hand of blessing and protection. Those who do the least for God always seem to expect the most from God. I mean, forget the fact that we disrespect God's name every day in our films, curse him in our workplace, ignore him 363 days a year, pay him lip service only on Christmas and Easter, deprive the poor, cheat on our spouses, and murder millions of babies in grotesque abortions. Come on, God, I demand my protection, my comfort, my security—my Happy Meals—just like I ordered. Every time we human beings think we know everything, we turn our back on God."

> *… in the last days there will be very difficult times. For people will love only themselves and their money. They will be boastful and proud, scoffing at God, disobedient to their parents, and ungrateful. They will consider nothing sacred. They will be unloving and unforgiving; they will slander others and have no self-control. They will be cruel and hate what is good. They will betray their friends, be reckless, be puffed up with pride, and love pleasure rather than God. They will act religious, but they will reject the power that could make them godly.* (2 Timothy 3:1–5)

Just watch or listen to the news and you'll see this scripture coming to life right before your eyes. That's probably why people say, "If you don't stand for something, you'll fall for anything." We can never forget that we are called to *love* and be the light shining for all the world to see. That's why God sent his son to die for us, and that's why he sent you.

No man knows how bad he is until he has tried very hard to be good.

—C.S. Lewis

TONKA'S TURD

From a young age, Chelsea enjoyed music. At around age ten, she asked me if she could download a song onto her iPod. She liked the song, but it had a bad word in it.

Shoot, she's been exposed to the songs teenagers listen to, I reflected. I talked with her mom and this is what we came up with. I asked Chelsea to tell me about the song.

"Daddy, there's only one bad word, but I won't repeat it. It's such a small part of the song. It's very little. I hear worse than that at school and I don't repeat it."

"Well, if you agree with me, then I'll let you."

"Really?" she answered.

"Okay, Daddy will make Rice Krispie squares for dessert and I'll add melted chocolate on top of it. Also, I'll put a small amount of Tonka's (our pug) turd in it. You won't taste it. It's very small, only a little."

She gave me a look like I was from another planet.

"Are you going to have some?"

"Noooo," she answered.

"Why not?"

"I won't eat Tonka's turd."

"It's a very small amount, Chelsea, and you won't taste it,"

She's smart; she got it. That song had a small bad word, and just like eating turd, it doesn't make it right just because it's a small amount. It's improper, offensive, and gross. Because the world exposes us to nasty things, we have a choice to let the enemy inside of us or to say *no*, it's not for me. The enemy fights with low blows; he is filthy, contaminated, and disgusting. He will try to slide in like a snake just to pollute our world. He wants us to sin and keep on sinning. When we allow Satan into our soul, he destroys us like cancer. Oh yes, if it's not acceptable for our kids, it's not acceptable for us. Would you listen to nasty lyrics or watch nasty movies in church or in kindergarten?

THE TALK

When Chelsea turned fourteen, we gave her a purity ring that she wore on her wedding band finger to symbolize her commitment to Christ until she gets married. We made a big deal of it. She had no clue. We got all dolled up and took her to a nice restaurant. I wrote two pages about the importance of purity in our generation and added some scriptures. I gave her the two sheets, and she read them. I wasn't sure if she agreed with what I'd written or not, but after she finished reading it she looked at us and said, "*Absolutely.*"

Karen and I were so happy! We explained to her that it wouldn't be an easy commitment, but putting Jesus at the centre of her life would make it easier. Then I presented her with the purity ring. I placed it on her finger, and she was ecstatic. To this day we have open conversations, and she still wears it. When she returned to school, some of her classmates looked down on her, and some were disrespectful when they found out what the ring represented. Was it jealousy, envy, or were those young people just hurting? I know from experience that sexual immorality destroys families and churches. It destroyed my mom and dad, and my sister and I were affected by it as well.

CHAPTER TEN

POWER OF PRAYER

If you are serious about your relationship with God,
you will find time to pray.
—Bill Hybels

A time of suffering is a small price to pay
for a clear view of God.
—Max Lucado

KAREN HAD BEEN DIAGNOSED WITH A brain tumour since 1988, and unfortunately had been given the news that it had grown quite substantially while she was pregnant with our daughter. Her doctor had prescribed her a particular medication, but she did not tolerate it well, so she stopped taking it.

All this ended any chance we had of trying for more children. But more importantly, I was concerned for my wife's health. I was a new Christian and my faith in God's power was growing.

For where two or three gather together as my followers, I am there among them. (Matthew 18:20)

I once heard this great acronym for the word "push":
P – PRAY
U – UNTIL
S – SOMETHING
H – HAPPENS

I took this acronym to heart.

I went to the head pastor of our church, Jay Davis, and asked if it would be possible, without Karen knowing, for the congregation to pray for her healing. That morning, she had been sick in bed with the usual nasty headache.

A few weeks later, Karen was not feeling well at all, so she was rushed to the hospital for tests, including an MRI.

After the tests were done, the doctor called Karen into his office to pass on the results. He was happy to tell her that the medication was working. Her tumour was in total remission. Karen was in shock. She told the doctor that she had never taken the medication, deciding that her quality of life was more important to her than the quantity. Once the doctor realized Karen wasn't on medication, he knew it had to be a miracle. She has been in remission ever since.

My whole family, and possibly my wife's also, believed that we were part of a cult because Christ had become the centre of our lives. How could we commit to a God that we had never seen? When we pray, we don't see our Saviour—just like we can't see the wind—but we can feel him. And we sure can see the end results of those prayers.

> Our whole earthly journey is like being in a storm, whether
> I want to admit it or not. I experience peace in the storm,
> knowing that I serve a God who can handle anything.
>
> —Unknown

By being patient, God uses dramatic methods to work in our lives. He doesn't expect us to be prosperous, but he expects us to be real and faithful.

Here's a good analogy. God knows how much I can tackle, and he challenges me. Faith is like a muscle; it grows with exercise, gaining strength over time. When I train or exercise, my athleticism increases. My muscles are developing, getting stronger and more powerful with resistance. If there is no resistance, the muscle won't grow or mature. In the same way, my faith has to be tested so that it can grow and become more intense and powerful.

> *For by grace you have been saved through faith, and that not*
> *of yourselves; it is the gift of God, not of works, lest anyone*
> *should boast.* (Ephesians 2:8–9, NKJV)

Before, I thought that being good to others and doing good deeds was enough for me to get to heaven. Good deeds are important to God, but they will not earn us eternal life.

I am the way, the truth, and the life. No one can come to the Father except through me [Jesus]. (John 14:6)

> There is absolutely nothing we can do or say that will bring us salvation. It is our belief in Jesus and relationship with God that will bring us there, not our acts.

The joy I experienced in our creator definitely did not come from man. The peace, love, wisdom, and blessings that he wants to shower us with are incredible. I had never felt this way before. I had to share what was happening to me with my old buddies. By their reactions, I could see that some were not open to it. They had too much pride to depend on God. They thought my faith was ridiculous.

Pride goes before destruction, and haughtiness before a fall. (Proverbs 16:18)

On the other hand, some were open to God and now they are experiencing the same blessings as I do. They saw the light and realized how they themselves were allowing the ways of the world to control them.

> It is amazing how those of us who are the most egotistical and self-centered are also completely unaware of it. It is always a good idea to ask a trusted friend or confidante if they see you teetering on the edge of conceit.

The difference I could see in myself and others was a decrease in ignorance and arrogance. Ignorance is the lack of knowledge, or being uninformed. Arrogance is having an excess of pride or vanity, maybe thinking God isn't big enough.

Jesus had a humble heart. If he abides in us, pride will never dominate our lives.

—Billy Graham

You can learn from God's wisdom or you can be dragged down by the weight of your own stupidity.

All the negative reactions and comments I got were not directed at me; they were directed at the Lord Jesus Christ. In the beginning, I took it personally. But they weren't really rejecting me … they were rejecting Jesus. Pride had done that to me before. The truth did bother me, and now I want to be right with God even if people see me differently. Jesus died a gruesome death on a wooden cross, and the best way to acknowledge that is for me to live well, even if I stumble sometimes. That's why I need him forever. For my co-workers and some friends, it's easy to blame God for all of the negative things in their lives. They certainly didn't make an effort to make this world a better place. I told them that real joy, real happiness are not found in bars or at the bottom of a bottle. I wasn't escaping the reality of this world anymore with drugs and alcohol.

If sometimes I get caught up participating in conversation about the old days of one-night stands, strip joints, and drunkenness, almost everyone joins in, bragging and laughing. I have to remember to guard myself against such worldly thoughts. If the subject turns to my relationship with Jesus, that's it, the conversation is over. There is no more interaction other than the occasional polite nod. I can see how ignorant they are of God's love, afraid to surrender their hearts to Jesus.

We still have to keep loving on them and trying to become more like Jesus. The big mistake we make is to compare ourselves to others or want to be like them. It takes a lot of work to pretend to be like someone else. We weren't created like them, so we can't be them if we want to grow to our full potential. If we don't love ourselves, how can we love others? Begin to love yourself now. You are awesome.

To remain on God's path, I ask him to keep me close to him. I tell him to hurt my heart if I hurt his. It's a great teaching tool. I know that I have to keep working on myself constantly. The Lord doesn't want any of us to hurt. We can't blame God if our heart is hurt by the world. People are hurting so much, they think that by hurting others back, they'll feel better. We all know that's wrong. Make sure you discern who really wants you to be miserable, because it's definitely not our Heavenly Father, Jesus Christ.

Jesus Christ isn't a favourite subject of my non-Christian friends. They probably think I'm crazy, but that's okay. I can feel their negativity and doubts. Following Jesus didn't make me very popular with my family and friends at times. I was often ridiculed. No one disrespected me to my face, but that's not always the case. Some will completely disapprove of and oppose your beliefs, and that's okay. God gave all of us a choice to follow or not.

I attended a Ravi Zacharias question and answer period in Toronto. One of his statements was: "We have the right to believe whatever we want, but not everything we believe is right." If we only knew how much God wants to be part of our lives.

I am a child of the most powerful God. Start believing what you say about yourself. The more you say it, the more you'll believe it, and the more you'll live it. Say great things about yourself, because you are a child of God.

When my friends notice a difference in me, that's when I know I'm doing the positive work God wants me to do here on earth. I definitely do not want to lose them as friends, so my actions must speak louder than words. One thing they cannot stop me from doing is praying for them, hoping one day we will all be on the same journey together.

And the judgement is based on this fact: God's light came into the world, but people loved the darkness more than the light, for their actions were evil. All who do evil hate the light and refuse to go near it for fear their sins will be exposed. But those who do what is right come to the light so others can see that they are doing what God wants. (John 3:19–21)

Many people don't want their lives exposed to God's light because they are afraid of what will be revealed. They don't want to be changed. Don't be surprised when these same people are threatened by your desire to obey God and do what is right, because they are afraid that the light in you may expose some of the darkness in their lives. Rather than

giving in to discouragement, keep praying that they will

come to see how much better it is

to live in light than in darkness.[3]

_____

[3] *Life Application Study Bible (New Living Translation)* (Wheaton, IL: Tyndale House Publishers, 1996), 1625.

CHAPTER ELEVEN

FACING RESISTANCE

Rejoice in our confident hope. Be patient in trouble,
and keep on praying.
(Romans 12:12)

LOVE IS A CHOICE. AS I grew more and more in love with my wife and precious daughter each day, I began to get angry at my dad. I couldn't understand how he could leave his own family for another woman. I couldn't dream of doing that to my own family. Many things had happened between me and my dad. After twenty-six years of broken promises and hurtful lies, I finally ended all communication between us.

I used to wonder why a loving God allows suffering. Most of the time, the suffering is the outcome of our own choices—for instance, drinking and driving, drugs, alcohol, pride, adultery, lies, lack of love, and greed. The lives we will have tomorrow obviously depend on the choices we make today.

My dad was now dating a woman who had won the lottery. I really felt that his love of money had replaced his love for his children. Dad was retired and always said he was too busy to come and visit, yet he found the time to spend four to six months in Florida every year. What was I supposed to think or say? His conversations were always related to money. In other words, he never had enough, but he never lacked anything.

> *For the love of money is at the root of all kinds of evil. And some people, craving money, have wandered from the faith and pierced themselves with many sorrows.* (1 Timothy 6:10)

Greed leads to all kinds of evil: marriage problems, robbery, blow-ups in partnerships. To master greed, you must control it at its root. Get rid of the desire to be rich.[4]

I wrote my dad a twenty-four page letter about how I felt not having a father figure in my life, how bitterness had set in because he was never there when I needed him.

Lots of mean words came out of my father's mouth; he had left them on my answering machine. I wouldn't accomplish anything by repeating what he said. Both of us were hurting, and yet I had to honour my dad, as it states in the bible:

---

[4] Ibid., 1935.

Honor your father and mother. Then you will live a long, full life in the land the Lord your God is giving you. (Exodus 20:12)

—————

It is of the utmost importance to show respect to our parents in our words and actions. But there is no requirement to submit to them if they themselves do not obey God.

—————

Karen and I had already purchased plane tickets to travel to my hometown that year for Christmas, to show off our new baby to my family. Sadly, after having such a big falling out with my dad, we cancelled everything and decided to spend the holidays with Karen's family, who lived closer.

Karen's family was very close, due to her loving parents. They were there for their kids, whenever or wherever they were needed. They always treated me with love and respect. During this Christmas celebration, I was hurting. I knew they couldn't understand everything that I was going through, but Nan and Pop really did their best by trying to remove the heavy load of pain I had in my heart. They kept the Christmas spirit at its highest and let me know they were there for me if I needed anything. There wasn't much they could have done; this was my journey to work through, but their effort was genuine and I will always remember it.

Being a Christian doesn't mean that we are perfect. I myself am far from perfect in my private life. I have temptations, and I have to pray and repent in order not to act on them.

... watch out! Sin is crouching at the door, eager to control you. But you must subdue it and be its master. (Genesis 4:7)

The devil never showed me a positive end. It's always negative. He is sneaky, powerful, and evil.

But when people keep on sinning, it shows that they belong to the devil ... But the Son of God came to destroy the works of the devil. (1 John 3:8)

I read somewhere that it's not the ship in the water, but the water in the ship that sinks it. So really it's not the Christian in the world, but the world in the Christian that constitutes the danger. We have to be aware of our surroundings.

Satan is waiting to destroy us at every turn. We are weak on our own but can fight back with the strength of our faith in God, as well as with other believers' prayers and encouragement.

People who make a habit of sinning will always find excuses to defend themselves.

In 2001, as reborn Christians loving the Lord, Karen and I decided to rededicate our lives to God by getting water baptized in front of our congregation. We wanted to do this so that we could be held more accountable for our actions, or lack thereof.

A COMFORTABLE CHRISTIAN

A comfort zone is a beautiful place but nothing ever grows there.

—Toby Mac

In the spring of 2001, I had yet another fight opportunity. I was asked to train four guys who fought in the cage and practised the sport of mixed martial arts.

I went to the head pastor of my church, asking about his thoughts regarding this type of fighting. Was it appropriate for a Christian?

He gave me great advice: "Stephane, pray about it."

It was that simple. I should always rely on God for answers, and I shouldn't worry about what others are thinking, just what God thinks.

In the fall of 2001, one of the guys I was training got a chance to fight for the Canadian Championship belt at the Ultimate Combat Challenge (UCC 6) in the middleweight division. This is where GSP, George St-Pierre, began competing in MMA before he became the UFC welterweight and middleweight champion. On the same fight card, the UCC was looking for heavyweights. They asked me if I was interested. I wouldn't commit 100%, and they were not even sure whether or not heavyweights would be on the card.

So I continued training the middleweight fighter for his fight, preparing myself as well, just in case the opportunity arose. I was feeling good, healthy, and injury-free. Two weeks prior to the fight, however, I ripped my elbow open during an intense training session, requiring twenty-five stitches. My chances were over, buried in the grave forever. My mind was at peace. I went to the tournament to be a cornerman. There was the answer to my prayer. My training partner lost, so he couldn't get the championship belt.

I am definitely not overly religious, but I do have a relationship with our Saviour Christ Jesus. UFC fighter Victor Belfort explained it best in an interview, when he said, "I'm not religious at all. I'm the opposite; I'm relational. If you're religious, you follow men and what men tell you about things. I am relational, because I have a relationship with the Bible."[5]

Don't trade your life for temporary things.

—Rick Warren

With all the wrong choices I have made, now I just want to follow what the Bible teaches us. Scriptures teaches us to be careful how we live, to make wise choices, and to make the most of every opportunity for doing good in these evil days.

> But since you are like lukewarm water ... I will spit you out of my mouth! (Revelation 3:16)

Allow God to light a fire in your heart. There is nothing more repulsive than a Christian who talks the talk, but doesn't walk the walk.

---

[5] Donovan Craig, "Miracle Mile," *Fight Magazine,* (December 2010): 61.

I once knew a comfortable Christian. What I mean by that is that he was firing up a 911-prayer only for what he wanted, and it was not necessarily godly. He usually cried out to God only when things were not going his way. I also call this the "cafeteria prayer." It's fast, easy, picking up a bit of this and a bit of that. You cannot just pick scripture that is comfortable for you. Example: I'll give to the poor, but I won't forgive my neighbour. See what I mean! That comfortable Christian sometimes made it to church for one hour each week. He would throw a few coins into the collection plate and exchange pleasantries with those around him, but it was never anything too demanding. This guaranteed that he could have the rest of the 167 hours in the week to fulfill his own selfish desires. He never wanted to get to involved, for fear of having to give up his own personal time.

We should be asking what Jesus wants of us, not what we want to do to fulfil our own desires. We have to do God's will in prayer, not ours—even if the prayer is completely opposite of what we want. Having a relationship with our Heavenly Father is free and a great way to live. The dictionary even says that prayer refers to thanksgiving, praise, and confession to God.

By the way, that comfortable Christian was me.

If any of you wants to be my follower, you must give up your own way, take up your cross, and follow me. If you try to hang on to your life, you will lose it. But if you give up your life for my sake, you will save it. And what do you benefit if you gain the whole world but lose your own soul? Is anything worth more than your soul? (Matthew 16:24–26)

THE US NAVY SEAL'S MOTTO IS "GET COMFORTABLE BEING UNCOMFORTABLE"

Opening our hearts to Jesus, putting our focus on Him, allows us to see what wonderful joys life really has to offer. Thinking we can do it on our own usually results in us making poor choices.

We can face any situation that comes into our lives. By being uncomfortable, we can go to places we may think unimaginable to serve Jesus. We can't serve God with one foot in and one foot out, like on a balance. That's why we see so many divorces today. As married couples, we get comfortable and complacent. We take our spouse for granted, getting caught up in a routine. We make time for what's not really important. We have to be all in. Jesus should be part of everything we do.

I used to tell people that I was passionate about Jesus, but when I removed my blindfold and saw where God stood in my life, I realized I was fooling myself. God helped me see that I was passionate about my personal training, MMA, and anything related to fitness. I was living for my selfish desires, comfortable in my bubble. Because I attended church, went to Christian conferences, said my prayers (sometimes), and helped friends, I honestly thought I was all in. But my actions didn't match my words. In Matthew 15, Jesus says that people honour him with their lips, but their hearts are far from him.

That was me. I had some knowledge about Jesus, but no relationship. Here's a similar story to Pastor Kyle Idleman's. I remember my mom hanging a picture of Jesus on my bedroom wall. On the opposite wall, I'd put up a picture of Guy Lafleur, #10 on the Montreal Canadiens. I knew everything there was to know about this great player. I knew where he was from, how many kids he had, and all his statistics. I didn't know the fellow personally; I had no connection to him.

Later in life, I became the same with Jesus. I knew where he was from, the many miracles he'd performed, and that he'd died a gruesome death on the cross to save the world. I knew the Bible pretty well too. I knew about Jesus, but I had no connection with him whatsoever. Again, my lip service was A+, but my actions needed major improvement.

Kyle Idleman in his book *Not a Fan* states that "many of our churches in America have gone from being sanctuaries to becoming stadiums. And every week all the fans come to the stadium where they cheer for Jesus but have no interest in truly following him. The biggest threat to the church today is fans who call themselves Christians but aren't actually interested in following Christ. They want to be close enough to Jesus to get all the benefits, but not so close that it requires anything from them."[6]

That's a great explanation of comfort. Jesus wasn't at the centre of my life. I spent more time studying *Fitness Magazine* or different martial arts disciplines than I did getting to know Jesus. I

[6] Kyle Idleman, *Not a Fan: Becoming a Completely Committed Follower of Jesus* (Grand Rapids, MI: Zondervan, 2016), 25.

was a master at partying. I also spent more time with my television remote control than in scripture or prayer with the Lord. My actions didn't always match what I tried to portray.

We've all heard the saying: "Nobody is too busy, it's a matter of priorities." Yes, I was too busy, but not the right kind of busy. I wasn't growing with Christ. God wants to see in us his spiritual fruits, not a religious freak. My talk was cheap, but it sounded good. Many of us still wear blindfolds and still don't understand the meaning of carrying our cross daily. James 2 tells us that faith without action is dead. If we say we believe, our actions should naturally follow. That comfort zone is killing us. Talking about my faith was one thing—now I had to live it.

Get involved wherever you are in your walk with Christ. Let's go one step further together today for the kingdom. Remember, God didn't promise a comfortable life, but he promised comfort and peace in him along our journey. We often put a wall up because we aren't comfortable with changes. Following Jesus requires us to put aside some comfort, and often rejection and persecution will come our way. Some even die for voicing their beliefs. Living for Jesus today may come at a hefty price.

Think of the soldier who went to fight for freedom and never came home. He gave it all; he didn't have comfort. When you leave this world, how do you want to be remembered? We all want a better world to live in, and it has to begin in us. The sacrifices we make often remove the comfort zone we allow in our lives. Hey guys, I still get caught up in this comfortable world, so you're not alone. Just say, "Jesus, guide me, lead me, and direct me where you want me" and step up and serve him. If the Holy Spirit leads, we will be open to change.

AM I TEACHABLE?

Around 2004, a friend of mine and his wife invited Karen and I to attend a seminar/conference on marriage and parenting with Dr. Kevin Leman, a well-known Christian psychologist, speaker, and author. I told him that our marriage was good, and we had a pretty good idea of how we wanted to raise our daughter in Christ. Full of pride, I said, "I'll pass. Maybe next time."

"Okay," Bob said, "I'll give you the money and you can teach me."

Wow … what a comeback! I didn't realize how little I really knew, and I wasn't teachable. I thought we were doing fine … but according to who? Suddenly I wasn't the expert anymore. After his pep talk, I realized that I didn't want to be just a good husband or just a good father. I wanted to be a great husband and a great father.

Coming out of my comfort zone that summer weekend was the best thing to happen to me and my family. Honestly, my career is only a job, but my faith is my whole life. Our priorities are often not in a good order. The question I ask myself is: "Stephane, if you're not just a little uncomfortable, are you really doing what God wants of you?" The Bible tells us all that God wants from us here on earth. Everyone who does God's work will face resistance of some kind. Because their hearts are all in, they're committed to serve. When we go all in, we can see the gift God gave us. He also gives us strength and courage to do what he requires. I just want to save *one* more for Jesus.

CHAPTER TWELVE

CHEERFUL GIVER

The way to live is by giving.
—Stephane Therrien

*"Bring all the tithes into the storehouse…" says
the Lord of Heaven's Armies … "I will pour out a
blessing so great you won't have enough room to take
it in! Try it! Put me to the test!"*
(Malachi 3:10)

THE GOVERNMENT DOESN'T TRUST US WHEN it comes to finances, so they take what they believe to be theirs before we receive our paycheque. God does trust us with our finances, that we will give back what belongs to him. Everything belongs to God. Heavenly Father, I am so grateful that love is tax-free. I would be penniless for all the love I have for you and the two girls in my life.

Wherever your treasure is, there the desires of your heart will also be. (Matthew 6:21)

Being a cheerful giver is about more than just dealing with money. It also concerns giving your time, helping the needy, volunteering for a good cause, and helping your neighbour. If they come from the heart, all these things are far better than donating tons of money with no thought except to receive a tax write-off.

There is nothing we own that has not come from the grace of God. Hoarding our blessings only proves how little we trust God to provide for us. Giving back is one of the greatest blessings of all.

I don't want to preach to you, because I also had some struggles with giving. I had questions regarding giving certain amounts of money to the church. We often hear stories on television and through the media about how money is mishandled, misused, or doesn't make it to its destination. Our pastor told us to pray that God would open our hearts and expect an answer from our Lord. Ask the Holy Spirit to guide you and give you wisdom to do God's will. God promises to provide for us. Remember that the blessings God promises are not always material and may not be experienced here on earth. God also asks us to be good stewards with our money.

Wise people know that all their money belongs to God.

—John Piper

We say that we trust God with everything. Here's an analogy. Trust is like money wrapped in a rubber band. When we try to pull it out of our pockets, the rubber band provides too much resistance and the money snaps back in. Or we're like Barney the dinosaur … our arms are too short to reach into our pockets to give. We just don't want to let go, but we have two cars, a boat, snowmobiles, a nice house, expensive clothes, and large screen televisions. I know we work hard for our money, and God wants us to enjoy it, but we need to have faith to trust him with our lives.

God gave us everything we have. You say that you worked for it, yes, but wait one second. God provided that job. That's our problem. We're so prideful, we think we're doing it on our own. Now that I know that everything is from God, we pray together as a couple before we spend anything. We wait for God's approval. If he closes the door, we don't insist on it being opened.

WE HAVE TO PRAY FIRST

I don't want to gamble with God. We trust and test him as to what he said in Malachi 3:10. I hear my family members, and some friends, gambling with God in prayer. They say, "God, if you answer my prayer, I will light a candle in church," or "If you give me this job, Lord, I'll start giving more." What are you doing with your money now? We have to believe and trust God with all aspects of our lives. It's a matter of the heart.

If I can't give God priority in my finances, he's clearly not the priority in my life. I can't say that I'm zealous for God but be unwilling to give back a portion of what he's provided for me.

I trust God and can name a few blessings that are not financial in nature. For example, my daughter is a miracle baby and my wife has been healed from a brain tumour. The Lord has removed many bad habits from my life: drugs, anger, drunkenness, porn, pride, hate, and sooo many more. He can do the same for you, if you let him. I have comfort in God's promises; when I let God control my life, I always end up in a better place than where I would be trying to do it on my own. When we realize everything that we have, we can appreciate and see how blessed we are and how all our needs have been met.

From a young age, I prayed that God would give me the right woman. I couldn't be happier with his choice. Because of this, I consider myself to be a rich man, and also because of the good friends I am surrounded by.

I choose to give my worries to him. Why worry about things I cannot change? If I cannot change them, I don't fret about it. I simply trust in God to help me through it. If I can change something in my life, I do so.

The bottom line is, we cannot pick and choose what the Bible tells us. If we keep trying to do life on our own, it means we don't think God is big enough for us, and we think that we are above him. Speaking from experience, I know that if you do not believe in our Lord Jesus Christ, you will believe in anything and worship everything but Jesus.

The paradox of our time in history is that we have taller buildings but shorter tempers, wider freeways, but narrower viewpoints. We spend more, but have less; we buy more, but enjoy less. We have bigger houses and smaller families, more conveniences, but less time. We have more degrees but less sense, more knowledge, but less judgment, more experts, yet more problems, more medicine, but less wellness.

We drink too much, smoke too much, spend too recklessly, laugh too little, drive too fast, get too angry, stay up too late, get up too tired, read too little, watch TV too much, and pray too seldom. We have multiplied our possessions, but reduced our values. We talk too much, love too seldom, and hate too often.

We've learned how to make a living, but not a life. We've added years to life not life to years. We've been all the way to the moon and back, but have trouble crossing the street to meet a new neighbor. We conquered outer space but not inner space. We've done larger things, but not better things.

We've cleaned up the air, but polluted the soul. We've conquered the atom, but not our prejudice. We write more, but learn less. We plan more, but accomplish less. We've learned to rush, but not to wait. We build more computers to hold more information, to produce more copies than ever, but we communicate less and less.

These are the times of fast foods and slow digestion, big men and small character, steep profits and shallow relationships. These are the days of two incomes but more divorce, fancier houses, but broken homes. These are days of quick trips, disposable diapers, throwaway morality, one night stands, overweight bodies, and pills that do everything from cheer, to quiet, to kill. It is a time when there is much in the showroom window and nothing in the stockroom.[7]

THE HOUSE FIRE

In the fall of 2004, we had a fire in the basement of our house. With our daughter fast asleep, Karen and I were just about to curl up, relax, and watch a movie together. It was damp and cold outside, so I decided to turn on the gas fireplace for the first time that season. It started up without a problem, but as soon as I returned to my chair, the power went out—not something terribly unusual in the neighbourhood.

I went looking for the flashlight in the furnace room and made my way to the electrical box to see what fuse had tripped. Nothing seemed to work, so I figured there must be a line down somewhere and power would return when they fixed it. As I returned the flashlight to its place, I happened to look up. Smoke was coming from the furnace area. I told Karen to get Chelsea out of the house and call 911.

---

[7] Bob Moorehead, *Words Aptly Spoken* (Seattle, WA: Overlake Christian Church, 1995).

God, in his grace, allowed Chelsea to sleep through it all as Karen brought her to a neighbour's house and laid her safely to bed. Once the fire was controlled and put out, the damage had to be assessed, but that would not take place until the following day.

In the meantime, just one phone call had friends coming to our aid. Before long, we had a place to sleep. Another good friend, Darrin (who played in the NHL, as described in an earlier chapter), came from another town to make sure we were safe and looked after. He had been looking for us until the wee hours of the morning. All we could think about was how grateful to God we were that all that was damaged was a house, and that our family had not been harmed at all.

The next day, we lived through a whirlwind of events, including phone calls to insurance companies and adjustors. We were put up in a hotel. At first it was for two weeks, but it turned out to be more than two months. Although the situation was not ideal, we knew we were blessed.

We tried to keep the same routine as much as possible, but it was difficult. However, God once again remained faithful in his promise to be with us, giving us comfort at every turn. Many people showed pity on our situation, but we looked at it as a bump in the road. We honestly had no fear or worries that God would not provide, and he continually did. People came and brought toys for Chelsea. We fellowshipped with other Christians who we might otherwise never have met, and then went on to become best of friends with them. With all the free time, due to not being in our own home, Chelsea spent a lot of time in the hotel pool. She eventually learned how to swim there.

The biggest lesson we learned was about our money. As they were doing the home repairs, we had to pick out so many replacement items. The insurance money was slow in coming and we really were not sure what they were going to cover sometimes, so we had to use our own resources. We were put to the test when we had to decide if we should continue to tithe or not—after all, doesn't everything belong to God anyway? After talking it over with Karen, we decided that we could not stop, and we would tighten up other areas before the one which was the most important.

> *You must each decide in your heart how much to give. And don't give reluctantly or in response to pressure. "For God loves a person who gives cheerfully." And God will generously provide all you need. Then you will always have everything you need and plenty left over to share with others.* (2 Corinthians 9:7–8)

Shortly after that decision, Karen received some pension checks that she had been unaware of. Each and every time we thought we were bone dry in our resources, it seemed we had a little windfall. We knew in our hearts that these blessings were no coincidence, that God in his goodness was more than providing for our needs.

It was so wonderful to come back into our home just in time for Christmas. More wonderful was the lessons we learned, lessons that came from trusting God in all his greatness.

CHAPTER THIRTEEN

A FRIEND AND MENTOR

Many books can inform you; only the Bible can
transform you.
—Author Unknown

THE BEST WAY TO KNOW GOD is by praying and learning the scriptures. God reveals himself to us through the Bible. His message couldn't be more obvious: it tells us the way it is.

People are afraid of the Bible because they know the Bible teaches right from wrong. We do not want to give up our favourite sins. It also tells us that doing good deeds or being a good person isn't good enough, that the only way to salvation is through Christ. The scriptures tell us what we need to know regarding Satan's purpose for us, his ideas, his strength, his downfall, and his capacity. It also instructs us on how to protect ourselves from Satan.

The Bible is like a military compass, acting like a map to help us find our way. The more I read my Bible and go to church, the more I understand the Word of God. It's just like reading the owner's manual to a new car. The more you read and understand, the more you enjoy your car. If God had never changed my life, I would not be spending my time getting ridiculed by friends or talking, telling, and writing about him.

Here are a few topics the Bible speaks about:

Love, faith, disease, marriage, good/evil, happiness, disobedience, joy, prayer, promises, hope, obedience, parenting, peace, strength, forgiveness, kindness, health, discipline, offering, tithing, sickness, behaviour, fear, money, comfort, poverty, suffering, jealousy, bitterness, lies, adultery, blessing, protection, idols, religions, prison, wisdom, divorce, selfishness, pride, anger, addiction, punishment, miracles, profanity, cults, salvation, alcohol, death, life, gossip, vanity, temptation, attitudes, repentance, eternity, grace, consequences of sin, physical exercise, relationship, fellowshipping, and natural disasters.

Do you understand why I do not need a library? You can address all these blessings and problems by talking, praying, and having a relationship with God through Jesus.

I wonder what would happen if we treated our Bible like we treat our cell phones. What if we carried it around in our purses or pockets? What if we turned back to go get it if we forgot it? What if we flipped through it several times a day? What if we used it to receive messages from the text? What if we treated it like we couldn't live without it? What if we gave it to kids as gifts? What if we used it as we travelled? What if we used it in case of an emergency? What if we upgraded it to get the latest version?

This is something to make you go, "Hmmmm… where is my Bible?"

Oh, and one more thing. Unlike our cell phone, we don't ever have to worry about our Bible being disconnected, because Jesus already paid the bill.

—Author Unknown

I was talking to a non-Christian friend of mine about the way he worshipped his favourite musical band. He attended nearly half of the band's concerts, travelling all over the world. He spent a good portion of his income on this. He told me that he idolized the band, and I laughed out loud.

A little insulted by my reaction, he said, "When I find out who you idolize, I'll laugh, too."

To which I quickly responded, "Jesus is the one I love to idolize."

"Oops, I won't go there."

He had respect for Jesus. If this guy put as much energy into worshipping God as he did into that band, what a great Christian he would be!

NOW FOR THE GOOD STUFF

You may be a (fill in the blank) expert, but what kind of Christian are you?

—Mark Buchanan

Karen and I began to strike up a friendship with our pastor, Bobby, and his wife, Heather. They mentored us, teaching us about having a relationship with God—how to pray, the Holy Spirit, fellowshipping, repenting from our sins, and believing even when it seems impossible. They taught us that Christians are not perfect people, that we still struggle although we know God is there to comfort and support us. When a car hits a pothole in the road, it needs proper care and alignment to function well and to go in the proper direction. It is the same for us. Sometimes God needs to realign and discipline us to go in the proper direction.

You say you have faith, for you believe that there is one God. Good for you! Even the demons believe this, and they tremble in terror. (James 2:19)

For all of us who call ourselves Christians, believing in God doesn't mean we are saved. The devil believes in God, but is he saved? Going to a boxing match doesn't make you a boxer, and going to church doesn't make you a Christian. The only way to heaven is with God through Jesus.

When I'm doing prison ministry and building relationship with the inmates, I tell them: "It's funny that we all want to go to heaven, but we don't want to do God's will here on earth." The scriptures are clear. We choose our destination, our eternity, by choosing God's Word or not. At the end, the Lord just honours the choices we made. We can't pick and choose the scriptures. The Bible says that *many* are called to spend eternity in heaven, but only a few will enter the kingdom of heaven. That's scary. What choice are you making? Today isn't too late if you decide to put Jesus at the centre of your life.

There is salvation in no one else! God has given no other name [Jesus] under heaven by which we must be saved. (Acts 4:12)

No other religious teacher could die for our sins; no other religious teacher came to earth as God's only son; no other religious teacher rose from the dead. Our focus should be on Jesus, whom God provided as the way to have an eternal relationship with Himself. There is no other name or way![8]

I used to be a weekend alcoholic. Alcohol was an addictive, controlling force in my life. I needed booze to have fun. Alcohol isn't a problem in my life anymore. I no longer get drunk. There were no good messages in the bottle… at least, none that I could hear. Now Jesus is my drug of choice.

Don't be drunk with wine, because that will ruin your life. Instead, be filled with the Holy Spirit. (Ephesians 5:18)

---

[8] *Life Application Study Bible (New Living Translation)* (Wheaton, IL: Tyndale House Publishers, 1996), 1695.

I feel I must humble myself here and share one of my worst addictions—my addiction to pornography. I could never get enough. I had viewed pornography since I was a young boy.

Drugs and alcohol are used to avoid life's hard choices, but only for awhile. It is a very self-indulgent way to live.

THE DAMAGE OF PORN

The temptations in your life are no different from what others experience. And God is faithful. He will not allow the temptation to be more than you can stand. When you are tempted, he will show you a way out so that you can endure. (1 Corinthians 10:13)

When I was ten years old, I went to the store, and the line to the cashier was long. I walked to the bookstand, where I encountered my first X-rated magazine. Pornography was hard to find back then, but now it's hard to avoid. It's a fantasy world that robs us of true, loving relationships.

My heart began to beat fast, and I became extremely excited. I stole the magazine. In one instant, my heart and soul became corrupted. I knew that what I was doing was completely wrong.

At ten years of age, I had experienced "fondling" with my eighteen-year-old babysitter. The next weekend, the same thing happened with her sixteen-year-old sister. I was hooked. I became addicted to sex and pornography. I viewed my dad's sex magazines every chance I got. As a young man, I was involved in hockey and boxing, and always meeting lots of girls. I was an example of what *not* to bring home to a mom and dad who wanted to keep their daughter pure. I was sexually active at a very young age.

When my girlfriend broke up with me, I turned to porn videos, and all my pain went away. From then on, I found pornography to be a great pain killer. It was like a merry-go-round of lustful images and impure thoughts. I was never faithful and never satisfied with just one girlfriend. At seventeen, when I travelled the world with the military, I became worse. I had no sexual morals. I definitely don't want anyone to treat or look at my daughter that way as she gets older, just like you wouldn't want anyone looking that way at your daughter, mother, sister, or even your wife. It's different when we look at it this way, isn't it?

When I was looking at pornography, I created fantasies in my head. I saw the people performing the acts as sex objects and definitely not God's creation. I was encouraging and supporting the porn industry and the humiliation and corruption of women. I was feeding my selfish desire. I was like a mummy on the inside—rotting—while I looked normal on the outside. The god I was honouring was pornography and anything that had to do with sex.

Porn opened doors for me to constantly cheat, lie, and use women. I was ashamed of even mentioning God's name. That's what the enemy wanted. I went to strip clubs until I was thirty-two. It got worse—I began working for Male International, which is similar to Chip & Dale (male entertainers), by organizing events for the ladies. I was engulfed with sin. If I wanted a future with Karen, it had to stop. I was still going to church every Sunday; I was a hypocrite. I listened to God's teachings but didn't follow them. Eventually, the Bible showed me the evil of my ways. I was poison, a real disgusting example to society.

Sin is everywhere. Satan preaches to all of us through television, school, work, beaches, restaurants, and other venues. We have to be ready to battle temptation. My whole life was a lie, acting nice to people while the real me was in darkness. I couldn't change the empty feeling on my own.

I will teach you wisdom's ways and lead you in straight paths.
(Proverbs 4:11)

In 2001 I was searching for God, hoping he would forgive me, and he did. I was praying and learning more about the truth, the Bible. The more I learned, repented, and prayed, the closer my relationship with Jesus grew. I was tempted less because I was relying on him more, and he always gave me a way out (when I asked). He helped me deal with the root issues in my life.

I read a survey conducted in 2016 that said 42 to 53 per cent of men in Canada believe that watching pornography, buying/selling sex, and sexually active high school students is morally acceptable. Sad.

Some temptations are so strong. It's best to be like a boxer and bob and weave, or dodge it like a soldier when temptation comes your way. Don't forget that Jesus is in the fighting ring with us. He's always with us on our battlefield.

It is well said that neglected prayer is the birth place of all evil. When we forget to ask God into our everyday activities, the devil comes in uninvited.

—C.H. Spurgeon

I am accountable to my wife. Karen knows everything about my past, from old girlfriends to old habits and temptations. She doesn't judge me. Just the opposite, actually; we pray for each other's weaknesses, handing them over to a powerful Lord. We have our computer out for all the family to see, with no hidden passwords. I have to be careful not to break those rules with a careless decision, otherwise the consequences will affect me and the ones I love.

Put on all of God's armor so that you will be able to stand firm against the strategies of the devil. For we are not fighting against flesh-and-blood enemies, but against evil rulers and authorities of the unseen world, against mighty powers in this dark world, and against evil spirits in the heavenly places. Therefore, put on every piece of God's armor so you will be able to resist the enemy in the time of evil. Then after the battle you will still be standing firm. (Ephesians 6:11–13)

Until I surrendered and turned to Jesus, I didn't experience satisfaction in anything I did. It all faded away. We cannot rely on man or earthly pleasures for joy, but we sure can rely on Christ for complete joy and satisfaction. I felt it when I put him at the centre of my life. However, I know I will always have resistance from the negativity that surrounds us.

The following chart contrasts the equipment and preparation needed to go to war as a regular, flesh-and-blood fighter and as warrior of God.

AS A FIGHTER...	AS GOD'S WARRIOR...
You need to study your opponent.	You need to study the Devil.
You need discipline.	You need discipline.
You need power.	You need the Holy Spirit.
You need to have a game plan.	You need the Bible.
You need to defend with your gloves.	You need to defend with your Shield of Faith.
You need a coach.	You need a pastor.
You need proper equipment and training.	You need your Helmet of Salvation, the scriptures.
You need focus.	You need your Belt of Truth.
You need prayer.	You need prayer.

Satan laughs at our words, mocks at our work, but trembles when we pray.

—Author Unknown

… upon this rock I will build my church, and all the powers of hell will not conquer it. (Matthew 16:18)

The rock on which Jesus would build His church has been identified as Jesus himself.[9]

Pastor Bobby gave me some good advice on how to cement a great friendship with others:
- Wrestle about the Bible.
- Pray together.
- Forgive each other.
- Fellowship together.

Bobby became a great friend and, through God, he helped me deal with the pain I had inside regarding my relationship with my dad. He taught me about our Heavenly Father, about going to him for comfort. The process was simple; all I had to do was talk to God like I did with any of my other friends, like he was sitting in the room with me, always ending the prayer with "in the name of Jesus Christ." I began to pray, believing and developing a personal relationship with our Lord Jesus. I didn't just pay him lip service; I truly believed and meant what I said.

[9] Ibid., 1441.

Sometimes when God doesn't answer our prayers, that's God's answer. It's not necessarily what we desire. Remember how I was praying to be in every one of those fights? But it was not God's will.

Unforgiveness is like drinking poison and expecting the other person to die.

—Unknown

If you forgive those who sin against you, your heavenly Father will forgive you. But if you refuse to forgive others, your Father will not forgive your sins. (Matthew 6:14–15)

———————
Asking for God's pardon is so much easier than excusing the faults of others.
———————

My relationship with my dad challenged my spiritual, emotional, and physical health. That's why I had to pray and study the scripture. And I wasn't alone. I received prayers and support from friends, fellow Christians, and especially my wife Karen. Sometimes I felt convicted and had to complete this journey with Christ. I didn't always show much grace. To this day, I still haven't mastered grace the way God wants me to. Karen, on the other hand, has so much grace.

At the beginning, I didn't ask God to help me forgive, because I was hurting too much inside. I just said, "God, you know how I feel about my dad. I give him to you. I need your help."

When I think about forgiving my dad, I really see how small an issue it was when compared to other people's stories. Corrie ten

Boom was an incredible Dutch woman who almost died in a Nazi concentration camp. In 1947, she recalled seeing a man in a Munich church after giving a speech. She spotted him from across a crowded room, and fear gripped her heart. She couldn't look at him in the church clothes he was wearing; all she could envision was the skull-and-crossbones symbol of his Nazi uniform from when he had been a concentration camp guard. She was haunted by memories of the concentration camp, the harsh lights, piles of clothes in the centre of the room, and walking by this cruel Nazi guard.

After the service, he stopped in front of Corrie, extended his hand, and complimenting her on her great speech of forgiveness. Corrie couldn't look him in the eye. She was paralysed with fear of being so close to this former guard. He confessed to being a guard at the camp, but he said he had since given his heart to Jesus. He longed for forgiveness, and now expected it from her. He almost begged.

"Corrie, will you forgive me?" he said with his hand reaching for hers.

The way Corrie describes it is, she was paralysed. She could not forgive him, as her sister had died in that camp. Would forgiveness bring her back? She couldn't do it. Her heart froze, but after silently praying to Christ Jesus for help and strength, the power of Christ electrified her with the courage to grasp his hand. Peace washed over Corrie, overwhelming her and bringing tears to her eyes.

Without further hesitation, she uttered one of the most difficult phrases known to mankind: "I forgive you." Then she wept. Corrie totally felt the strength of God's love and the power of the Holy Spirit like she had never felt it before.

I couldn't let my pride control me. I chose to see my dad as how human he was. I don't think Dad understood the ramifications of his actions in the lives of my mother, my sister, and me. I made the decision to leave everything in God's hands, and suddenly I was set free from being a victim.

My friend Heather used the analogy of a bird to help me forgive my dad. She said, "If a bird poops on your shoulder, are you going to go after the bird or forget about it? It becomes your choice. If you let it go, it may stain your shirt for a while, but it will eventually fade away. But it won't totally disappear. My point is that you may never forget about the incident, but you have to forgive. If you don't, you will always hurt from that past experience. You have to let it go. You can learn from it. All of us have been hurt from someone, whether it be at church, work, school, or by family or friends. If you want to live, you have to forgive."

Forgive others, and you will be forgiven. (Luke 6:37)

We must love ourselves first to be able to love others. Real love isn't about pleasing myself. It's about pleasing God first and placing the needs of others above my own. I gotta be careful, because sometimes my selfish desires come first, and then I catch myself.

With prayer, patience, and encouragement from Karen and Bob, I gathered myself together. I hadn't spoken

Those who show grace have also received it.

with Dad in almost four years, but in December 2005, without any animosity or grudges, I called him. My heart was beating fast. I was almost hoping his answering machine would cut in.

But it didn't.

"Hello," he answered.

"Hi, Dad. It's me, Steph. Please hear me out and don't interrupt until I'm finished." It felt so good to talk to him. "Dad, I forgive you and I love you. I want to share how I felt all my life and how I missed you not being there for us. I know this is the right thing to do."

I told him about all the hurtful things he had done to my mother, my sister, and me. This has helped me to become a better husband, father, and warrior of God.

> *... you must clothe yourselves with tenderhearted mercy, kindness, humility, gentleness, and patience ... forgive anyone who offends you.* (Colossians 3:12–13)

Knowing how much God loves us enables us to show love and mercy to others.

My dad told me that he hadn't had a father figure in his life to learn from. We talked for over three hours.

Before I hung up, I said, "The bottom line, Dad, is that I missed having a father figure in my life, to talk with, share, learn from, and laugh with. I accept you the way you are." I've learned that forgiving others doesn't mean I trust them more. It's not selfish, but I have to forgive so that the healing process starts for me. It's also a command from God so that I can move on with my life. When I hold on to bitterness, I can't help others. We can't forget also all the good things they've done besides that incident. I'm sure that I rub people the wrong way more often than not.

He heals the brokenhearted and bandages their wounds. (Psalm 147:3)

Now God has healed my heart.

CHAPTER FOURTEEN

OBEDIENCE

*Trust in the Lord with all your heart; do not depend
on your own understanding. Seek his will in all
you do, and he will show you which path to take.*
(Proverbs 3:5–6)

Love and kindness are never wasted. They always make a
difference. They bless the one who receives them and they
bless you, the giver.

—Barbara DeAngelis

I WOULD LIKE TO SHARE with you one
of my experiences when I let God's Holy
Spirit take charge of my life. I prayed
that his will be done, not my own.

*When you reach out to
God, you will receive
all the protection,
guidance, and direction
you need.*

Here's how it happened. I was shopping for a new SUV. My old one had high mileage and years of hard work behind it, so it needed to be replaced before I had to pour lots of money into it. I had been looking around at different car dealerships and searched the internet for deals.

Dave, an old friend of mine, came to mind, as he was the owner of a local car dealership. Dave was one of my old buddies that I went barhopping with on the weekends. We had lived in the darkness together; Satan definitely had a hold of us.

Thankfully, Dave had seen the light and become a faithful follower of Christ with his family. He and I had voluntarily sinned and served the fallen angels of this world, and now with God's grace and power we still had something in common—now we served the all-powerful loving God of the universe.

I called Dave and told him what kind of vehicle I was looking for and he told me that he had something different that I may like. I trusted Dave, so we spent forty-five minutes on the phone. I was excited, but wary. I wasn't sure if this is what God wanted for me.

"Dave, I am very interested," I said, "but I know I'm not doing the right thing. I have to pray about it first. I would like you to pray that I make the right judgement call, and I'll ask Karen to do the same. I'll get back to you."

"No problem, Bo-Bo" he responded. His tone of voice was the same. There was no animosity. Dave may have lost a sale, but not a friend. I knew he respected God's decision.

Ask me and I will tell you remarkable secrets you do not know about things to come. (Jeremiah 33:3)

We prayed by asking God to help us decide. At 4:00 a.m. the next morning, I woke to go train at the gym before work. I had received an answer. I was excited, because God had answer me very clearly. I couldn't even focus on my training. At lunch break, I called my wife.

God loves us and wants to pour his blessings upon us, but we have to ask. With God, all things are possible. He is so much bigger than us. We have to understand that we are not able to achieve our full potential by depending on our own strengths.

After a brief exchange, I asked her the big question: "Did you get an answer regarding the SUV?"

"No, not yet. Have you?"

"Yes, I did!"

"Are you buying it from Dave?"

"Nope."

"Where then?"

"Karen, it makes so much sense. God answered me clearly! I can't be wrong with this one. It wasn't a dream or my feelings; it was an answer to my prayers."

"Tell me then."

"She doesn't know yet, but…"

"Who doesn't know what?"

"We have to buy a car for my sister. Remember, her car broke down three weeks ago."

Now listen to Karen's reply: "If God gave you that clear of an answer, that's what we have to do. Being obedient is the way to honour the Lord Jesus." Live, love, respect, honour, and pray together. If you do, you'll have a marriage made in heaven.

You can pray for anything, and if you have faith, you will receive it. (Matthew 21:22)

By being obedient, I know Jesus was proud of us. I had seen a very reliable car that my sister would enjoy, and it was even in her favourite colour.

As our relationship grows with God, we tend to pray for Godly blessings as opposed to selfish desires. When it is God's will, He delights in granting us blessings.

I went to the dealership and negotiated the price with the general manager. By the time we were done, it was getting late. I was the last one finalizing paperwork that evening. The manager offered me a deal for my old truck, trading it in for the exact SUV I had originally wanted.

"Sure," I said. "But only if you give me a better price for my sister's car and buy my truck at the price I want to let it go for, so that I can afford the payments on the SUV without being short on cash."

"No problem," he agreed.

"Can I talk it over with my wife for a few minutes?"

"Take your time."

Before contacting Karen, I called somebody I knew who had the same SUV as the one I was about to purchase. I wanted to ask him what he thought of his car. After all, he had bought it from the same dealership.

He answered the phone. "Hey, Steph. A car dealership number is on my call display."

"Yes, I'm at a car dealership now," I said. "I have to be quick. Do you like your car?"

"I sure do, it's my second one. Who's in the office with you? Are you buying one?"

"The guy's name is Andrew."

"He is a Christian, let me talk to him. He is my work associate's brother-in-law."

They talked for a few minutes. I was exhausted from all the emotion. What was I doing buying two cars in one day?

Andrew hung up the phone. "I didn't know you knew Paul or went to the same church."

"Hey, I didn't know you were a Christian, or that you knew Paul either."

Everything was happening so fast for me and I knew God was part of this deal, too. So I told Andrew about the car for my sister Manon, and how God had instructed me to buy her a car. He wrote down some numbers.

When all was said and done, I left the dealership with a car for my sister at a great price. I sold my truck for the amount I was asking for and bought myself the SUV I wanted with all the bells and whistles at a stolen price. If I wouldn't have taken the time to pray, asking and doing God's will, I never would have gotten this fantastic bargain... not to mention a clear answer from our Father in heaven.

What does it take for people to turn away from this dark world? The truth of Jesus Christ is right there in front of us. I convinced my sister to come and visit from Montreal. When she got to Ontario, I brought her to the dealership and parked in front of her new car. I got out and sat in the passenger seat, and told her to sit at the wheel of her new car.

She didn't believe me. Her reaction was priceless. She was overwhelmed. For sure, I was her favourite brother now, even if I was her only brother. What my sister didn't understand was that I was the blessed one.

PRAYER REQUEST

I've learned that when I pray, I want God to answer my prayer. We want God to hear our requests.

Life gets ahead of us. We're so busy with work, sports, entertainment … you name it. We only spend a little time in prayer, and we don't even take time to listen to God in return. We don't go to a quiet place to listen to the Holy Spirit. We're not still; we keep on with life. How can God get our attention if we don't make time for him? Again, I'm using myself as an example. I have many flaws, but thanks to my Heavenly Father's grace, he's still working on me.

I can be so stubborn sometimes. When we hear a car horn beeping, we know the car is close by. It gets our attention. The same applies to Jesus. What would it take for us to spend some quiet and quality time with him? For me, I have to wake up thirty to forty-five minutes earlier to begin my day with him. My mind is fresh and clear; otherwise, I find excuses and I don't put him first. God isn't a crutch, guys.

Let's stay focussed. I pray for wisdom, guidance, and protection for me and my family daily. I pray to do his will, not mine anymore. I ask him to prepare us for the new day he's given us. I ask him to help me understand what I'm about to read in the Bible so that I can absorb it like a sponge. The more we know the scriptures, the more we have to apply. If we don't read and spend time with God in prayer, how do we know that what we're doing is what God wants us to do? I'm done with giving lip service; I let my actions speak for themselves.

Sometimes God may answer my prayer through other people, or I may hear something. I have to listen and be alert and meditate on him. If I drive to New York, I'll need to look at the map before I get to my destination, not when I get there. I need direction from our creator before I start my day to see where he's going to lead me.

I was coming back on a Sunday from speaking at a church in Syracuse, New York with my family. Chelsea must have been around twelve. After my speaking engagement in the morning, the pastor prayed for protection and safe travels back to Canada and through the borders. He prayed that it would only take ten minutes to cross into Ontario.

We got to US customs in the evening, and the line up was as big as when we'd crossed a few days earlier. I picked a line behind countless cars and trucks. Well, who was on her watch at the border? Yep, Chelsea.

"Dad, I'm starting the clock now." Chelsea was excited. By the time the ten minutes had expired, we were in Ontario. The only thing Chelsea talked about for the rest of the drive was the prayer request that morning. Believe me, we had a green light to talk about how real God is. God says to ask him anything according to his will. The prayer was answered. How seriously do we believe he will answer our prayers?

Keep on asking, and you will receive what you ask for. (Matthew 7:7)

_____

Always solicit what you need from God. He will grant your needs to do His work.

_____

CHAPTER FIFTEEN

VISIBLE BUT UNNOTICED

Those who shut their ears to the cries of the poor will
be ignored in their own time of need.
(Proverbs 21:13)

It is not the man who has too little but the man who
craves more that is poor.
—Seneca

I LOVE GOING TO DOWNTOWN TORONTO with my family. A few years ago, we went quite often with some friends. Every time our daughter saw a homeless or less fortunate person, she asked for some pocket change or food to give. She always received a smile back or a "God bless you" in return. We could see her heart beaming every time she helped someone, so we made sure that we always had change or food to give.

After we'd made the trip a few times with friends, the husband, whom I'll call Pete, said to me, "Why are you giving money to those guys? You can't save them all." I just smiled. Then we saw another man sitting on the subway vent to stay warm. Of course, Chelsea grabbed my hand and looked at me with her big, brown eyes. Her look said that we couldn't just ignore him, so she gave him some pocket change. She received a "thank you" or "God bless you" as usual. Pete asked me the same question again.

I looked at him and said, "I bet it will make a difference to him."

My daughter's heart is as big as a house. If I walk by a homeless person and don't do anything, can I really say I'm living my faith? Friends, our actions should be done with our hearts, not to get the attention of others or a pat on the back, lest we become self-centred. Jesus said to us in Matthew that when we give to someone, our right hand shouldn't know what our left hand is doing. This means that our motives need to be pure and from the heart. The best question we can ask ourselves is: "Why do I give?" Make sure you give from a pure heart. As soon as you post it on Facebook, your reward in heaven is gone, according to the scriptures.

Imagine that less fortunate person as your own child. Would you advertise your deeds to the world? How far would you go to help? Never underestimate an act of kindness. We may never see the end results, but kindness represents love, and we need more love in this world today.

Here's a little story I heard once: A man had a dream that he was talking to Jesus.

"Jesus," he said, "why are there so many poor and homeless in the world?"

Jesus looked at the man and said, "I was going to ask you the same thing."

The moral of the story is that if we want the world to change, it has to begin with us. Helping someone becomes a choice of the heart.

Why is my heart with the poor and homeless? I asked God to stretch me out of my comfort zone even more than before. Then I had a few surgeries and was off work and in rehabilitation. A guy I knew was doing some work with the homeless at the time, so I asked him if I could go along and help. After working with him, I was haunted by those beautiful people down on their luck. I was troubled by their stories. I was also uncomfortable because these guys have *real life* problems. They need love and attention like all of us. To this day, it still bothers me that so many are homeless and we ignore or don't see them. It could happen to any one of us.

Having a daughter, my eyes welled and my heart was broken looking at those teenagers who should have been in school. They didn't seem to have a chance in life. I've heard people say, "Well, that's their choice." Honestly, *no one* wants to be homeless. Most people living on the street come with a series of unfortunate circumstances that brought them there.

Here are some possible triggers that led to their homelessness: Some have problems with drugs or alcohol. Some are divorced. Some have mental issues or are sick or disabled and require professional attention. Some end up in prison. Some were evicted by family members or landlords. Some were abused at home, so the street is actually safer. How sad! Some have bills much higher than their income, and some may have lost their jobs.

Everyone has a story, even street people. We can't pretend that we don't see them, because they're here among us. I met some great people with whom I became friends—people who'd spent a quarter of a century inside a prison cell. There were broken, just like me, but had different stories. They are still children of God.

I challenge you: The next time you walk by a person living on the street, smile and say hello. Your interaction could prevent a suicide. Offer them a coffee, or something to eat. Just care for them. Imagine people looking down on you if you're down on your luck. We should treat them the way we want to be treated. Just a small gesture could make someone's day. We won't get poor helping others. We will feel richer inside.

Investing in people will take some of your precious time, but the reward of helping others is amazing. Don't take my word for it … do it. Being generous to others without anyone around you is so exalting. If you've never done such a thing, you need a change of attitude first. You can begin by doing a small assignment like letting someone go first in line at the grocery store. Make a commitment to do one good action daily to make our world a better place. By doing so, we also change people around us, then some will do the same.

It could even become contagious in your family. It's our job to teach our kids those good actions. One good way to start is to teach them to give some of their toys away to the less fortunate.

Make it special for them by bringing them with you as you deliver the toys to a shelter. Let your kids give the toys to other kids. Then they will start to understand at a young age the pleasure of giving. Oh ya … don't forget to do it with a smile. Jesus taught us that when we give, we really find happiness. It's more of a blessing to give than to receive.

If we focus more on helping others like Jesus taught us, we won't have time to envy what others have, and we'll be satisfied with what God has given us. We're called to serve. I have the honour to do it at the David Busby Centre. Their slogan is: Helping Others Help Themselves. The Executive Director, Sara Peddle, and her keen staff work countless hours to improve the lives of those less fortunate. They help low income families, the working poor, youth in tribulation, and seniors who are struggling financially. If you're interested in helping, please contact me.

It's a place where people experiencing homelessness/poverty (we call them "participants"), or those in danger of becoming homeless come for help. It's not judgemental, just helpful. The Busby is a warm place, a safe haven, and for some, it gives them hope. Participants come for a shower and personal hygiene, exchange their wet or ripped clothes for donated clothing, have a coffee and some food, and get assistance in finding a permanent place to live so they can apply for jobs. All things we take for granted.

When I go and serve, I stop and chit chat with participants. Just like Jesus washed the feet of those he sat with, now I have the honor of cutting hair for the less fortunate. It's a very humbling experience.

They want to be heard. Some of the people I work with in the centre and in prisons know that I follow Jesus. They are some of the most honest people I've ever met, as they have nothing to hide.

Some of them have told us that Christians are fake. They don't mind Jesus, but they say we act like we have it all together, which is definitely not true. When they ask Christians how they're doing, they usually hear "good," "awesome," or "great." But that is only a façade to hide our pain. We're all in need of Jesus. We need to be more honest and real. Following Jesus is the hardest thing I've ever done, and the biggest hope I've ever had.

We can't pretend to have it all together. As Christians, we don't have it all together. We should talk about our flaws and be transparent instead of focusing on our positive traits. It's okay to tell others that without Christ, we are weak. It's okay to tell them that the Holy Spirit helped us overcome addiction, or healed our marriage. If we want to bring more people to Jesus, we can't sugar-coat the Bible. I say it the way it is, in love. I know some don't like it. My mouth isn't a bakery; I don't sugar-coat the scriptures.

Often street people or inmates will say things to me like "I don't know how to be a dad; I'm addicted to porn; I committed armed robbery just to survive; I stole a car; I always get into fights; I always end up in prison." They aren't afraid to talk about their life and expose their weaknesses. What you see is what you get with these defenceless people. I've discovered that if we share with others what the Bible says we are, more people will come to church and get to know Christ. Let's not pretend that we're great every time someone asks us.

OUTREACH TRUCK

Another one of my favourite ministries is the outreach truck. The Busby Centre also goes out into the streets with a truck that was given to us by the City of Barrie. It's an older ambulance that goes out seven days a week from 3:30 p.m. to 10:00 p.m. all over Barrie and surrounding area.

There are always two of us in the truck, and we assist participants who can't make it to the centre but need help. The less fortunate have a hard time securing housing because of increasing costs, which becomes a major problem. Homelessness is difficult; it's not a nine to five job, but a gruelling 24/7 time on the streets. In snowy weather and on rainy days, these people are still living on the street, so we're there to attend to their needs. They are hungry, cold, sick, and at times confused. Next time you're cold, think of them and say a prayer. They are tired and weak, but they keep on going because they want to survive. If you see someone pushing a shopping cart or looking dirty on the streets, don't look down on them. They are human and God's creation—bleeding, breathing, and hurting like all of us. They are somebody's friend, family member, or child … hopefully not yours.

Homelessness in Canada is increasing. I had the sad honour of speaking with some military veterans who are now living on the street after serving their country overseas in Afghanistan. Because of injuries such as PTSD, they can't find work. Helping the most vulnerable will always be a sign of love.

Jesus tells us: "*For I was hungry, and you fed me. I was thirsty, and you gave me a drink ... I was naked, and you gave me clothing*" (Matthew 25:35–36). He goes on to say that when we refuse to help the least among us, we refuse to help him. In 2017, between eleven thousand and thirteen thousand people used the outreach truck. That's a lot of emergency lunch bags! The bag includes one sandwich (usually made and donated by caring people), one juice, one granola bar, and one water. In the truck we also carry first aid supplies and gently used clothing, bedding, and hygiene products—even toilet paper, which most of us take for granted. Counselling is also provided. We have season-appropriate donations in the truck all year long.

Thank God that in Canada we have a program called "Out of the Cold." Between November and April, from 6:00 p.m. to 7:30 the next morning, the churches in the downtown areas of participating cities open their doors for street people to come in for a warm supper and to spend the night. It's made possible by donations and volunteers.

Remember the movie *Home Alone 2*, in which Kevin McCallister ends up in a different destination than his family? He goes to Central Park in New York and talks to a homeless lady caring for pigeons. They become friends, and she tells him that the birds are also her friends. She explains that people just pass her by. They see her but ignore her, wishing she wasn't part of their city. But everyone wants to be seen and heard.

The next time you come in contact with street friends, show them love and kindness by not ignoring them. Here is a poem

written by one of my friends, Whitey, who was homeless but made
it off the street:

HOMELESSNESS: No Fun at all
HAVE you BEEN HOMELESS OR SPENT YEARS IN JAIL
AND HAVE NOWHERE TO go
you THINK you HAVE Alot OF FRIEND
BUT THEIR TRUE COLOURS REALLY SHOW
you CANT FIND A PlACE SO you DITCH A TENT
WHERE you THINK NO ONES AROUND
SOONER OR LATER DOWN THE ROAD
you'RE BOUND To BE FOUND
THE CITY COMES IN TELLS you To VACATE
THEY THINK THEY'RE SO ROUGH AND TOUGH
BUT IF you DONT LISTEN To THEM
THEY COME AND TAKE ALL your STUFF
OR THERES OTHER CAMPER OUT THERE
WHEN your NOT THERE THEY LOVE To STEAL
IT DOESNT MATTER WHAT IT IS
your CLOTHES, BlANKETS, SHOES, EVEN A MEAL
you HAVE A BEER WITH ALL your BUDDIES
WHICH IS ALWAYS QUITE ALRIGHT
BUT DONT DRINK AS FAST AS THEM
CAUSE THERES ALWAYS A DRUNKEN FIGHT
THOSE PEOPLE BRING ON THE COPS
WHICH NO CAMPER REALLY NEEDS
ITS ALL OVER ALL THERE GREEDS
So IF you HAVE A PlACE ALREADY
WHAT EVER you DO DONT LOSE IT
NO MATTER WHAT IT TAKES
CAUSE ITS your LIFE, you CHOOSE IT

I GIVE my GOOD FRIEND STEPHANE
PERMISSION To USE THIS IN HIS BOOK   WHTEY
        WHTEY   2008

Chapter Sixteen

COMPASSION FOR THE FORGOTTEN

… whenever we have the opportunity,
we should do good to everyone …
(Galatians 6:10).

For those with no time, don't make excuses
—make a difference.
—Rob Horsley

IN THE FALL OF 2011, I was sitting in church beside my wife, who was involved in a quiet conversation with the lady beside her. It turned out that the girl she was whispering with was Christine Eisses, the president of Emmanuel's Wish Foundation, a Christian organization that not only talks the good talk, but acts as the hands and feet of Jesus to the hurting world. They work at slowing down the cycle of poverty from being passed on to the next generation. They do this through education, employment opportunities, and empowerment in Richmond, South Africa (S.A.).

After the service, Christine shared with me that she wanted a pastor to come to S.A. for a men's conference, but the Lord put it on her heart to ask me instead, as broken as I am. We didn't even know each other prior to this Sunday morning. Wow! She was very obedient to listen to God's voice and follow up with me after. She asked if I knew someone I'd like to travel and share the gospel with to this forgotten part of the world.

I told her that I'd pray with Karen for guidance from the Lord. I asked the Lord to clear my schedule if I was supposed to be in South Africa in March.

I had another surgery, my recovery time terminated, and then I took some vacation time from work and went to S.A. with my friend from Calgary, Pastor Bobby Thirsk.

Before leaving, I read a story from S.A. that traumatized me. It was about a fifteen-year-old girl who was in charge of her sibling after her parents died of AIDS. Twice a week she walked three hours each way to get drinkable water, carrying the heavy load on her shoulders/head. One day on her way back, three men approached her and violently raped her while a ten-year-old watched from far away. The men saw the young boy and forced him to rape her also.

I was afraid to go there. That girl was somebody's daughter. On top of that, I'd just received an email from Christine regarding a dozen young women rescued from a brothel after been repeatedly raped over a period of three weeks. I really didn't know what we were in for.

On March 17, 2012, I left for the unknown across the globe. I'd be speaking on the following topics:

- What does Jesus say about sex? Good and bad sex.
- The consequences of our choices. Where is God when bad things happen?
- My testimony and what it means to be a real dad today.

I made a quick stop at JFK, New York, and picked up Bobby. It was great to reconnect with the guy who to this day challenges me in my walk. After twenty hours of travelling, we landed in Johannesburg. Then it was on to another plane ride to Durban and a ninety-minute car ride to Richmond.

WAITING TO DIE

March 18. Still no sleep. Christine brought us to the hospice where we met patients with HIV/AIDS who were waiting to die peacefully. The hospice is equipped to serve those sick and dying. It's a comfortable place for them to spend their last days here on earth. Some can return home healthier to be with their families. The hospice brings dignity and hope to those afflicted with AIDS.

I met two ladies who had just escaped from the brothel, and both were on heroin wanting to detox at the hospice. I spent time with two little orphan children, Tondaka (girl) and Talent (boy), with AIDS. They were clinging to me, looking for love. I was sad, and it made me appreciate Canada even more. We live in one of the richest countries in the world.

We walked to a small trail in one of the poorest places in S.A. to get to the mud hut, a 10 X 12 little house made of mud. The roof was made of corrugated metal with holes in it and palm tree branches. It was held down with rocks all over and there was garbage all around the perimeter. No bed, no water, no electricity, no toilet, and two to three family members lived in there. They were happy, friendly, and smiling. The bed consisted of cardboard and a blanket. Clothes covered the mud floor. I'm a little ashamed of the way I think sometimes. In Canada, we wonder about what colour of paint to put on our wall, or what type of shoes to wear. These people wondered if they'd even eat or drink clean water each day.

We took two children with us that were malnourished. People from the little town became hostile, wondering where we were going with the children, but Scotch, our translator, told them we were getting help for the children. Bobby carried a naked child with a skin condition all over his body. I carried a five-day old boy with a major infection. His eyes were shut with dry puss, and he was so weak, he didn't whimper. The father of the child had never held or touched his newborn. I was the first man to give love and comfort to him. Staring down at the baby, I thought about my daughter and how lucky she was. Not even five days later, due to the care those children received from EWF, they were acting like healthy kids.

Everything that is done in the world is done by the hopeful.

—Martin Luther

March 19. Bobby and I went to a pre-school (daycare/nursery school) called Siyethemba (See-ya-tem-ba). It was named after a very special ten-year-old boy who'd stayed at the Comfort Home and was the first child to pass away from AIDS there. EWF Hospice and the children's centre was named in his honour. Siyathemba is Zulu for "We have hope," as we believe everyone should.

The children's centre serves forty to fifty children aged two to five daily from 8:00 a.m. to 4:00 p.m. The majority of these children come from vulnerable homes and were neglected or abused. Every day we'd show up to play with all the kids. We felt like rock stars, the kids made us feel so wanted. They jumped all over us. They wanted to be picked up, their thin little arms stretched out in the air. We played catch, hide and seek, and tickling. For me, it was definitely one of the highlights of the trip.

Most of these beautiful children never had a man's attention. It was a special day for them and us. We can't forget that our kids also need attention and not distraction. We say kids are bad with cell phones, but some grownups are worse.

Many foster homes were funded for children unable to be placed in a permanent home. Emmanuel's Wish also provides many other great services, like spiritual care, Bible reading and prayer, doctors, medicine, food, vitamins, and rehabilitation from drugs or other sickness. This care is provided on a 24/7 basis, but it cannot happen without generous help.

ANYMOSITY TO FORGIVNESS

March 20. Christine set up a conference with about twenty pastors who hadn't talked to each other for the past ten years. There were so many differences and much pride. They didn't look at or speak to each other, but because we were from another country, they agreed to come to listen and learn. We could feel the brokenness and pride in the room. In the morning, my topic was "Absent, Present, and Intentional Father." For lunch we had a small bite to eat, but still no one was talking to each other. In the afternoon, I spoke on "The Difference between Immature and Mature Christians."

Bobby is so real and gifted when he speaks. A miracle was coming. He led the last session of the day with the topic "Communication, Scripture, Prayer, and Fellowship/Forgiveness." All the pastors knew about communication, and they knew the scriptures inside out. But they only knew it. Prayer wasn't a problem, but fellowship/forgiveness was the reason they hadn't spoken for the past ten years.

After Bobby finished speaking on forgiveness, Pastor Peter got up and spoke in the Zulu language to all the pastors for a few minutes. He then proceeded to go around the room and hug all the pastors and ask for forgiveness; soon all the pastors were hugging and forgiving each other. It was the beginning of the healing process. Bob and I looked at each other in disbelief. We smiled and teared up a little. We were witnessing a miracle of love and forgiveness from God right in front of our eyes. It was surreal.

Following that, every pastor worked together setting up tents for the weekend men's conference. They also prayed and ate together. You had to be there to see it. They set up tents in a field beside the squatter camp, where two hundred South African men came and listened to the gospel Bob and I preached. Believe me, it was nothing fancy.

March 21. Still couldn't sleep. It was so hot and humid. We showed up at the hospice and painted the children's orphanage. It came back to life. Plus, we did a huge clean up around the property. We were beat. At 4:00 p.m., the first man I'd met when we arrived died. He weighed less than eighty-five pounds. Earlier, while we were cleaning, all the staff were praying and singing around him. There was lots of emotion during the last few days, and I was burnt out.

March 22. We had time to look at our notes for the conference the next day.

March 23. We delivered a very convicting message about the consequences of our choices. It was pitch black outside. No light or hydro. On our way home, we were followed by a truck. When we got to our destination, we got blocked in. No one was coming out of the truck. Obviously, some didn't like to hear that raping was wrong, even if their witch doctor told them it's okay. We needed security to get into Christine's place.

Saturday, March 24. This was the day they buried the dead. It wasn't as busy at the conference. It was a memorable day. After we finished presenting the gospel, many men came forward and prayed the salvation prayer. To wrap it up, all the pastors prayed for us. I always love it when people find out the truth about our saviour.

Sunday March 25. I spoked at a church that was so alive for Christ. In the congregation, I saw girls who had escaped the brothel a week prior. Now they were in church, praising Jesus. It was cool because they played the Canadian and South African anthems to show that we were united together in God. Following the church service, we flew back home.

I arrived home the next afternoon and surprised Chelsea at her school with Karen. I hid behind the wall, and when she saw me, she ran over and gave me the biggest and longest hug I'd ever had from her. Before I'd left on the trip, I'd recorded myself reading a nighttime story to her for each night I'd be away. Just a reminder that I didn't forget about my Carebear.

THE SLUMS

I also went on another mission trip in Nicaragua, where we visited a few schools. I brought along hundreds of erasers for them to use. Before handing them the eraser, I told them that I hadn't always followed Jesus. Before surrendering my life to him, I'd left many bad marks on the Book of Life. When I accepted Jesus into my heart and asked for forgiveness, Jesus *erased* all my sin, and my page became a blank sheet. I explained to the kids that God can erase all of our sin if we ask him to and repent, but we have to mean it.

We tried to go into the prison to speak with inmates, but we couldn't get in because of the lack of immigration papers. We were stuck with two hundred meals we'd purchase for the inmates. Our translator, Melvin, suggested that we could go and feed people living in the slums, who only make a couple of dollars a day collecting plastic bottles and metals. The smell was unbelievable. I can't fathom people living like this. Kids as young as three were collecting garbage for a living. They should have been in school. When they saw us coming with the food, they all rushed to get fed. I will never forget that day.

SELLING YOUR BODY

The next day, we went to New Image, a home for women being rehabilitated from sexual exploitation, or as we call it, prostitution. It's a place of safety for girls who were forced into prostitution by their boyfriends. New Image is a Christian organization that also helps children of women in prostitution.

Some parents send their kids out before they become teenagers to sell their bodies to get an income for the family. If they don't bring money home, they get beaten up. I don't want to be sarcastic, but tell me how bad our lives are now.

A good paying day for a street lady in Nicaragua brings in $1,000 cordoba, the equivalent of $40 US/day. I met Reyna, the fifteen-year-old daughter of a prostitute. She shared her sad story with us, and I was floored. I told her that all people, even friends and family, will disappoint each other, but Jesus will never disappoint us. She began to cry and told us that her family was never satisfied with anything she did. I asked her if I could pray for her, and she nodded yes. Tears ran down her cheeks. I began to cry as I prayed for her. Crying to the Lord for help, I thought about her tough life. I told her that Jesus healed my heart, and he could do the same for her, if she let him. Before leaving, I gave her a rubber bracelet that said: "I AM SECOND," meaning Jesus comes first. She gave me a big, long hug and smile. I told her that her family loves her, even if they don't show it sometimes. I felt like a father wanting to love another child I didn't even know.

> Poverty is the result of alienation and inequality and the selfishness and greed in our own heart.
>
> —Unknown

Early 2018, I had the chance to go on a humanitarian trip with our daughter and her school in Munoz, the north coast of Dominican Republic (DR), where they got hit by hurricanes Irma and Maria in 2017—one catastrophe after another. They were without electricity for days, and structures that toppled down still remain in that condition today, more than a year later. Munoz is a border town to Haiti, the poorest country in the Western Hemisphere. We worked with a Christian lady named Caitlin, originally from Virginia, USA. Caitlin had been there since 2016, and she founded Project Esperanza, which means "hope." It serves the Haitian immigrant population in

Puerto Plata in the areas of education, social aid (orphans), and community development.

The project helps the Haitians get back on their feet so that they're better equipped to go back to their own country and help others. A school teacher gets paid seven thousand pesos a month, which equals to $145 USD. The lead worker in charge of his crew would make one thousand to twelve hundred pesos a day, equal to approximatively $20 USD a day.

We were there at the farm to help build the pigpen and the green house. The school was very dilapidated, but it's considered a privilege to attend. We painted the classroom and worked on the exterior surrounding, preparing it for new cement. The working conditions were poor at best, as there was often a foot of mud to wade through, but the students faced each challenge with a positive attitude. We had twenty students with us who had to raise their own travel funds, and we brought forty-six hockey bags full of clothes, medicine, sports equipment, and other items, which we distributed in small isolated villages called "Batey." These are communities where the Haitians live, since they are discriminated against by the Dominicans. Their birth certificates are taken away so that they can't go back to Haiti, so they have to make their own communities. Due to the level of poverty, the people were overwhelmed to the point of almost fighting to receive something. As they received items, joy and gratefulness were written all over their faces. The poverty of Haitians living in the DR is one of the UN's top priorities.

CHAPTER SEVENTEEN

UNDER CONSTRUCTION

What we do in life echoes in eternity.
—Maximus from *The Gladiator*

ALMOST FOUR YEARS PASSED AFTER I forgave my dad, but I still did not see him in almost eight years.

In 2009, my dad's brother Camil (the uncle I was the closest to, who acted as my dad, friend, and confident, and whose door was always open to me) passed away. I attended his funeral. When I saw my dad there, it was still awkward between us. There were no feelings between the two of us. We only talked to each other for a total of five minutes.

> When you stop caring about church, those around you, and their hurt, pain, and needs, you have already begun walking away from God.

At the wake, Chelsea wanted to know who her grandfather was. Out of all the people there, she was able to pick him out. The last time my dad had held his only granddaughter had been in 2001. She had no memory of him.

In February 2010, my grandmother (my dad's mother) passed away. She was going on ninety-three years and was a great godly example for all of us for how we should live our lives.

My dad was very upset at the loss of his mother. Even though I had forgiven him, our relationship was still very cold. We only engaged in small talk. I knew God was speaking to my heart, however, so I made a big step of faith and asked my dad if he wanted me to go home to support him through this difficult time, to show my respect to my grandmother.

I stayed at his house for five days, and during that time I was able to reconnect with him. I loved taking care of him. I felt God's presence with me the whole time.

During my stay, I shared with him how much our Lord Jesus Christ had changed my life, how peaceful and joyful I felt. Better than that, Dad and his girlfriend told me when I left that they could see God's work in me, especially by my actions. My job was to plant the seed of God's love in their hearts, but only God could make it grow. I told them that they, too, could have this life, if they wanted it. It was their choice.

Preach the word of God. Be prepared, whether the time is favorable or not. Patiently correct, rebuke, and encourage your people with good teaching. (2 Timothy 4:2)

We should always be ready to serve God in any situation, whether or not it is convenient. Be sensitive to the opportunities God gives you, but no matter how much the truth hurts, we must be willing to listen to it so we can more fully obey God.[10]

Since my grandmother's funeral, Dad had been involved with me and his only granddaughter by calling, writing, and even visiting us. Our relationship was finally back to where God wanted it. I was extremely happy. That only lasted for a couple of years. Then he became distant again. Now I guard my heart by keeping it as a healthy relationship. My father hasn't changed much, but he is still my father and we are called to love, so I love him. We don't see each other much, but that's okay.

I see my mom every year, and our relationship is fantastic. My mom gave her heart to the Lord in 2016. We love having her around. She also has a servant's heart.

Work willingly at whatever you do, as though you were working for the Lord rather than for people. (Colossians 3:23)

Knowing that I am working for God makes everything more enjoyable, removing the boredom of life. People won't see your work when they're absent, but integrity, honesty, and

---
[10] Ibid. 1943.

strong moral principles even when people aren't watching are so important.

Imagine yourself as the child you were. What would that child think of you now and the person you have become? Is there room for improvement? I would think that there's always space for improvement. Today is not too late to begin.

Karen and I have been working for God. We have been interviewed for a Christian radio show and an internet program. We also speak in churches and I became the director of the men's ministry in our church, called Band of Brothers. At present, Karen and I serve in many areas of our congregation. After making an appearance on *100 Huntley Street*, I prayed for God to show me a way he could use me to do his work. I wanted to do something that would challenge me, some way that I could make a difference. When I arrived home, I received a call from my friend Pastor Bob. He wanted me to do prison ministry. It is wonderful how God speaks to us through the Bible, church, and other people.

I was sick and in prison, and you didn't visit me. (Matthew 25:43)

Talk about an answered prayer! I have now been doing prison ministry since 2006. Four hours a week, me

We must treat people the way we would like to be treated. We have a responsibility to help those in need.

and a couple of God's other warriors visit a maximum security jail up north to talk about our Saviour, the Lord Jesus Christ. We bring light and hope where only darkness reigns. To us, they are hardened criminals who deserve to rot in there, and maybe some should, because some of their actions seem unforgivable. But who are we to judge? That's God's job.

We are all subject to man's laws and punishments. But we shouldn't kid ourselves; we are all also subject to God's judgement. What about us? The sins we commit on a daily basis have become part of us. We don't usually acknowledge that we are lying, gossiping, cheating on our taxes or spouse, stealing, abusing power or using intimidation, constantly complaining, and thinking that the world owes us something. These sins may not seem as drastic or vile as those of the prisoners, but remember—to God, sin is sin. Some sins have bigger consequences than others, creating a snowball effect that keeps getting bigger and bigger.

If you think you are too important to help someone, you are only fooling yourself. (Galatians 6:3)

Not one of us should feel exempt from the responsibility of helping our fellow man.

Our little carebear Chelsea has retired from competing and instructing in Taekwondo after thirteen years as a second degree black belt. Now eighteen, she obtained her National Lifeguard Certificate and presently works and instructs in that field. She is studying to become a firefighter. Our greatest pride, in spite of all the things she has accomplished so far, is that she loves and serves the Lord. I often tell Chelsea that if she is extremely successful in this world but doesn't walk with Jesus, then it's all in vain.

God is using me to plant his seeds with my family, friends, and whoever wants to hear. Now they know they can find strength and comfort in Jesus Christ instead of doing it on their own. In our lives, we choose not to have any bad days. Life can be hard, difficult, and challenging—but because God is on our side, bad days are gone. In our family, there are no excuses—only obstacles to overcome. When I wake in the morning, I have to choose if I will be happy or miserable. If negativity comes my way, am I going to have pity on myself or learn a positive lesson? Guess what? I choose to surround myself with positivity. If negativity comes my way, I have to choose to absorb it or let it go. Don't allow someone else to dictate your mood. After all, it's your choice. If you think positive in life, you will lead a positive life.

> We can always second guess ourselves, but we cannot underestimate the impact of our choices. One choice can produce lifelong consequences for good or bad. Serving God will not always be the easy choice. But it is a choice that brings the kinds of consequences we can live with.
>
> —Bill Crowder

At the end of our journey, I believe God will ask us this question, because we are accountable for our actions: "Why should you be here with me in Heaven today?" Do you know how to answer? Are you ready? Because you cannot fool God. Being good isn't good enough. In Ephesians 2:8, Paul says we are saved by grace through faith in Christ Jesus. Please don't take this life for granted.

I saw the dead, both great and small, standing before God's throne. And the books were opened, including the Book of Life. And the dead were judged according to what they had done, as recorded in the books, according to what they had done... all were all judged according to their deeds... And anyone whose name was not found recorded in the Book of Life was thrown into the lake of fire. (Revelation 20:12–13, 15)

Imagine it this way. Suppose you are found guilty of a crime. You are in a courtroom in front of the judge, and he sentences you to death for your crime. His sentence is just. You are guilty, and the punishment for your crime is death. But suppose that judge is your father. He knows the law; he knows that your crime demands death. But he knows love; he knows that he loves you too much to let you die. So in a wonderful act of love, he stands and removes his robe and stands by your side and says, "I'm going to die in your place."

That is what God did for you. The wages of sin is death. Heaven's justice demands a death for your sin. Heaven's love, however, can't bear to see you die. So here is what God did. He stood and removed his heavenly robe. He came to earth to tell us that he would die for us. He would be our Saviour. And that is what he did.[11]

---

[11] Max Lucado, *He Did This Just for You* (Nashville, TN: Thomas Nelson, 2000), 46–48.

For this is how God love the world: He gave his one and only Son, so that everyone who believes in him will not perish but have eternal life. (John 3:16)

CONCLUSION

AS I LOOK BACK, REWINDING THE film of my life, I can see why our Creator has his time and place for everything. He has it all planned out, why things happen the way they do. All the special people who shared my life had a purpose and reason for being there. I can see the purpose for my military career and the various jobs I had, as well as the unanswered prayers regarding competing in fighting tournaments. I can see why I experienced the struggles, hurt, pain, and emotions of my fatherless life.

Most of all, I see the joy of knowing God through Jesus, of the gift of my marriage and our miracle daughter Chelsea. I'm also grateful for all the faithful friends that share my life. I am so blessed!

If you are still unhappy due to your life choices, the way it's going, feeling empty all the time, always wanting earthly desires and never feeling satisfied, I challenge you to develop a personal relationship with God. Don't just pay him lip service, but mean it from the bottom of your heart, surrender all to God, and pray a prayer of salvation (like the one in Chapter 9. Millions of people's lives have been transformed when they put our Lord God first. I am a walking testimony to this. God has a purpose for everyone. What is yours?

Throughout all this time, God has been moulding me. So if I make mistakes, don't be too quick to judge; I am not where I'm supposed to be yet. Our Heavenly Father still has me under construction.

And I am certain that God, who began the good work within you, will continue his work until it is finally finished on that day when Christ Jesus returns. (Philippians 1:6)

God has a purpose for you, and He finishes everything He begins.

RECOMMENDED READING

Stephen Arterburn, Fred Stoeker, with Mike Yorkey. *Every Man's Battle* (Colorado Springs, CO: Waterbrook Press, 2000).

Casey, Carey with Wilson, Neil. *Championship Fathering: How to Win at Being a Dad* (Colorado Springs, CO: Focus on the Family, 2009).

The Holy Bible

Groeschel, Craig. *The Christian Atheist: Believing in God but Living as if He Doesn't Exist* (Grand Rapids, MI: Zondervan, 2011).

Idleman, Kyle. *Not a Fan: Becoming a Completely Committed Follower of Jesus* (Grand Rapids, MI: Zondervan, 2011).

Cpl. Nathan Justice. *Path of the Warrior* (Winnipeg, MB: Word Alive Press, 2010).

Kevin Leeman. *What a Difference a Daddy Makes* (Nashville, TN: Thomas Nelson, 2000).

Teigen, Rob and Joanna. *A Dad's Prayers for His Daughter: Praying for Every Part of Her Life* (Ada, MI: Revell Publishing, 2014).

Rick Warren. *The Purpose-Driven Life* (Grand Rapids, MI: Zondervan, 2002).

White, Joe. *Fuel: Devotions to Ignite the Faith of Parents and Teens* (Colorado Springs, CO: 2003).

Robert Wolgernuts. *She Called Me Daddy* (Carol Stream, IL: Tyndale House, 1996).